INSIDE ALLEGANY

Volume I

TO MY SONS
TECK, JESS AND NICK
BEAHAN

INSIDE ALLEGANY

Volume I

LARRY BEAHAN

COYOTE PUBLISHING OF WESTERN NEW YORK
5 DARWIN DRIVE
SNYDER NEW YORK 14226
LARRY_BEAHAN@ROADRUNNER.COM

2012

COPYRIGHT 2012 LAURENCE T BEAHAN MD
ISBN 978-0-9703104-4-7

INSIDE ALLEGANY: VOLUME I

CONTENTS

PART I: PEOPLE

GEORGE HERON
PRESIDENT OF THE SENECAS

HOOK FRANCE
OF BAY STATE

JEFF RUPP
SECOND ALLEGANY STATE PARK
PATROLMAN

JUDGE LANCE ANDERSON
 LAW SOUTH OF THE ALLEGANY

JOE OLIVERIO
1940'S ALLEGANY BAND LEADER

JOHN "JUMBO" FELLOWS

PART II: PASSIONS

HOT DOGS AND MARATHON SKIING
LARRY BEAHAN

ALLEGANY CHRISTMAS STORIES
ALLEGANY HISTORICAL SOCIETY

ALLEGANY HOOTENANNY
SALLY MARSH

ALLEGANY SKI JUMPING
TED LACROIX

MAPLE SYRUP
WAYNE ROBINS

CHOIR CAMP AT CAMP CARLTON
ALFRED KARNEY

SPORTS CAR RACING ON RED HOUSE LAKE
BRUCE PERRY

PART III: <u>PLACES</u>

ALLEGANY FIRE TOWERS
LARRY BEAHAN

ELLICOTTVILLE
FOOTHILLS TRAIL CLUB

WOLF RUN
DEBBIE MINA

RED HOUSE INN
CHARLIE DACH

BUZZARDVILLE
PAT AND BERNIE SHEFFER

CEMETERIES IN THE PARK
HUGH DUNN

VILLAGE OF CATTARAUGUS
PATRICK CULLEN

PART IV POLITICS

LOGGING

GAS

JULY 2009
APPEAL TO PARK USERS

ACKNOWLEDGEMENTS

This two-volume book was made possible by the Allegany State Park Historical Society in its enthusiastic pursuit of old Allegany hands to relive Park history for us. The willingness of those Park denizens to tell their stories was the absolute essential ingredient. I wrote down what they had to say.

Thanks go to the Allegany State Park Administration for providing meeting space in the Red House Administration Building and the St. John's-in-the-Woods Chapel where these stories could be told in the setting of rustic cabins, rippling lakes and forested hills, where in fact they happened.

Photos were generously loaned by the Buffalo Museum of Science, Seneca Nation of Indians Fish and Wildlife Service, Buffalo State - Courier Express Collection, Bob Byledbal, Bob Schmid, John Phelps, Rick Feuz, Lyn Beahan, Wayne Robins, Edna Northrup, Sally Marsh, Ted LaCroix, Alfred Karney, Bruce Perry and Paul Lewis.

My sincerest thanks to you all.

Larry Beahan

INTRODUCTION

Inside Allegany is a collection of stories told by people who love Allegany State Park. They worked in the Park; played here, some were born here. The book is divided into two volumes simply because one would be too large. The division also serves to roughly divide the stories into earlier and later. Each volume has four parts: *People, Passions, Places* and *Politics*.

Allegany State Park is 60,000 acres in size and close to 100 years old. These two volumes give you only a glimpse at all that has gone on here.

PREVIEW VOLUME I

The *People* section of *Volume I* allows several Allegany characters to introduce themselves. George Heron worked with the Civilian Conservation Corps in the Park, later was elected president of the Seneca Nation, and led the Seneca protest against the Kinzua Dam. Hook France, a former Park Ranger, was born and still lives in the Park as is the case with Red House Town Justice Lance Anderson. I'll let you discover the other characters.

Passions refers not only to the many relationships that have blossomed in the Park including my wife Lyn and my honeymoon as camp counselors but also to all the varied activities people have loved doing here: ski-jumping and ski-racing, singing at Hootenannies and in choirs, telling stories around campfires, making maple syrup and, believe it or not, racing sport cars on frozen Red House Lake.

Places: The land comprising Allegany had a long history before it became a State Park. Fascinating remnants of that history are hidden in its forests and under its lakes, including cemeteries, building foundations and oil wells. Our steel Summit Fire Tower served to protect the Park for years but now, as a relic, it provides a wonderful view. And close by are the colorful nineteenth-century communities of Cattaraugus and Ellicottville.

Politics, many of us prefer to forget about politics when we escape into the woods. This section takes an opposite tack to look at threats to Allegany State Park and what we can do to protect the Park.

PREVIEW VOLUME II

The *People* section of the second volume of *Inside Allegany* begins with Seneca storyteller Midge Dean Stock. I love her story about how Rabbit got so ugly, especially since she admits it is hard to believe. Bob Byledbal ran concessions and dancehalls in the Park. Next time you see him, ask him to sing the Cornplanter song or if he really told his staff to tell customers, "Those are raisins, not flies, in the ice cream."

Mercy Holliday was a waitress at the Red House Inn. She tells the amazing story of her aunt's obedient pet turtle, Toots. Women are more evident in Volume II. That may justify the cover photo of campers in 1920's swimsuits at the old Quaker Run Mud Hole. I like to think of them as the Ziegfeld Follies Girls.

Passion: People are passionate about bears. Dick Roth covers black bears for us and naturalist Wayne Robins teaches us about the many other mammals encountered here including coyote, raccoon, beaver, fox, squirrel and the rare and vicious fisher, an animal that can spin around inside its own skin and bite an attacker. Seneca snow-snake-maker Michael Crouse initiates us into Snow Snake, a sport in which a stick is thrown at amazing speed and travels down an icy trough for a mile or more.

Places: Bob Schmid attempts a synopsis of the whole history of the Park. Pete Smallback takes us on a tour of a section of the Friends Boat Launch which used to be his family's farm and before that was Tunesassa, the Quaker

Seneca Indian School. Paul Lewis leads us to the ruins of an Irish immigrant settlement in Red House. And the Seneca Fish and Wildlife Service show off their Steelhead Trout and Allegany Hellbender (giant salamander) rearing installations.

Volume II's *Politics* section brings us full circle. It describes the new Allegany State Park Master Plan signed into law in 2011 that protects the Park from lumbering and mineral extraction and guarantees that it will be there as we know it for a good long while.

Whatever your passions, I wish you a great time at Allegany, the best Park in the world.

PART ONE

<u>PEOPLE</u>

GEORGE HERON
PRESIDENT OF THE SENECAS

March 2005

George Heron, in his ninth decade, moved slowly toward the podium. He leaned on his cane, glanced up and gave this aside, "I'm not so agile as I was when I was working up on high steel." The sixty people gathered in the Red House Administration Building great-room gave him a chuckle and a hand.

George Heron 2005

George had been president of the Seneca Nation in the 1960's when the Kinzua reservoir flooded a third of the Nation's Allegany Reservation. He'd also been a steel construction worker, a teacher, a member of the CCC, (Roosevelt's Civilian Conservation Corps,) and a veteran of the Pacific and European theaters in WWII. Framed against the French windows, with the snow-covered lake to his back, he began "This place is very familiar to me and I see a lot of familiar faces. Our State Park Band used to practice in this room, Luther Jimerson, Jim Carr, Floyd Printup. They played *Lazy Bones* and *Wagon Wheels*. Bob Remington had the big tuba. They were a bunch of Indians and farmers but they made sweet music together."

Motioning toward the great beams that support the ceiling he said, "Clarence Watt and Lewis Jimerson cut those hand-hewn timbers."

Seneca Band
Courtesy of Buffalo Museum of Science

"CCC Camps 50 and 51, sister camps, were on a side hill near here. Veterans Camp on the Quaker side was sold to the Catholic Diocese and became Camp Turner. We built the Stone Tower up at the Summit. The CCC ID or CCC Indian Department built the steel tower over on the reservation. They lived at home and came to work for eight hours. I belonged to the regular CCC. They had to haul the steel across the river in a flat bottom wooden john-boat. They had a horse named King they used to haul the steel up the hill. The horse was very popular over to the reservation. The tower is still there, on the reservation. So they can't very well tear it down.

Civilian Conservation Corps cutting pole for a fence

"The camps were run by army officers. City boys came to work in them and many stayed on. They supposedly took only the qualified unemployed. I was 17. They asked my name and age. I never had a birth certificate. All we had was a Council Certificate that you were born at Elko or Coldspring.

Later years started going to hospitals to get born. Neighbors off the reservation started going there, too.

"I worked two years in Camp 51. I did interior carpentry work on those three-room cabins on Ryan Trail. Went back up there to hunt Ginseng. Against the law but I got away with it. I know every nook and cranny of the Park.

"After the War, Warren Brothers constructed the road over to Quaker. All the gravel came from John Sharp's pit here in Red House. He'd stand there and watch his farm disappear. It was fine ground gravel. They'd mix it with oil to form a mulch and called it black top. Road work provided a lot of employment for local people from over to Bay State. We had an old Model T with a box on the back. Called it a 'Runabout.' We used to run up the Bradford Road with it.

"I went to a Quaker meeting in Philadelphia once to ask for help against Kinzua Dam. The first part of the meeting was silence. Everybody sat there thinking. Then someone got up and confessed, 'I thought ill of so and so.' People got up and spoke. They had a 'Stated Clerk' wrote things down. At the end of the meeting the Stated Clerk got up and read the consensus. There was no voting yes or no. I was amazed at how the meeting ran.

"We always got along with the Quakers. They built the Quaker School at Tunesassa. That name was cut down from a Seneca word, joh nis si yo, that means 'good gravel.' People couldn't say the whole word. If you were an orphan you could go there. After while others went, too. They had their own pig farm. Did their own slaughtering. Taught animal husbandry. Lee John was 12 years old. The school superintendent came by, saw him harnessing up a horse. He said to Lee's father, 'I wished you'd send him to the school to help with our horses.'

"Some stayed on for high school and then went to college or normal school. My mother went to normal school and became a teacher. She taught in Old Town. The school still stands. But before that she worked in Chilocco Oklahoma where she married the Irish–Pawnee shop teacher. So I have one grandmother that was born in Ireland.

"But intermarriage was earlier than that. Cornplanter's father was a trapper from Albany. I'm six generations down from Peter Crouse who was a Dutch captive from Fort Pitt. They took him home but he came back and married Tippani whose mother was a witch. They had ten kids, five girls and five boys.

"I am a master of the Seneca tongue as it was my first language. Taught it seven years in high school after I retired. I used to work on the Erie Railroad 'Extra Gang' from April to September. There were thirty of us and we all spoke Seneca, all except the foreman. He'd complain 'Too much diggedy-dog here, too much diggedy-dog'.'"

George made signs with his fingers, like a wagging jaw, the way the foreman had mocked them. "When I got home from the war, Aunt Jennie greeted me. We'd talk Seneca all day."

"In Seneca, some long phrases we make short:

(I'm sticking my neck out here because George did not stop to give the spelling of these Seneca words.)

'Wow' means 'He put it in the water.'

'Tide' is 'He did it on purpose.'

'Ees' means 'All of you.'

"Our alphabet has 16 letters. We use 'K' instead of 'C'. We got the "ell' out of our language long ago." He paused for a laugh on that one. "We have no 'R's' but the Mohawks and Onondaga's do, from the French influence.

"The first Indians the French run into were the Mohawks and Onondagas so those tribes became Catholic. We call them 'He who makes the cross,' or 'The person who wears black.' Baptists we call 'They dunk them in the water.' They used to do that down in Red House Crick, sometimes when it was cold. Even non-members, we'd go down to watch," he said with a grin. "Episcopals, we call 'Long Skirts.'

"Some call the Longhouse religion old. But it's not. We had European Churches earlier. Between 1795 and 1805 Handsome Lake had his visions that got Longhouse started. Thirty-five percent of Senecas follow the old, old religion, Gaiwio, the Good Word.

Allegany State Park Indian Cabin
Courtesy of Buffalo Museum of Science

At the Presbyterian Church, we used to have 135 people, no more. They came from all over. Now I go for brunch. But Holy Cross Church has a hundred cars. Catholics are more church people. I married several times, once to a Catholic woman.

There is Seneca medicine called 'little water medicine' and they use certain bandages. It never cured anyone. They should go to the doctor. The Good Lord gave us penicillin and antibiotics. They have the burning of tobacco. An old chief told me once, 'Always burn tobacco first or there may be trouble. Burn tobacco before you tap a tree or dig a root.' So I do, just to be safe, just to be safe. My daughter raises my tobacco now.

"I have been talking to an Anthropology class. I been going a long time. The students change. They used to be Jews from New York City and a big mix. Last time, half the class were oriental, Chinese. Never-the-less, they were interested and paid attention to my talk about Senecas. I talked for an hour and twenty minutes and didn't collapse."

At this point George picked up a framed photograph. "This is my aunt and uncle, Mr. and Mrs. William Bomberry. Notice the willow branch bench they are sitting on." Next he handed round a notebook with an American flag on the cover. "I have compiled this book about the 114 Seneca WWII Vets who have died. There were 128 originally. There is Shongo, Redeye mixed with all kinds of other names. Seneca names now are a roll call of the United Nations.

"My niece is a Kozlowski. She's an adventuress. Went up to Alaska to teach. Moved on up the coast till she got to Point Barrow. She married the Indian agent there. They adopted two Eskimos and now they all live in Steamburg and still get their Alaska oil pipeline checks.

"Well, I'm just about out of steam," George said, looking as if he was ready to give up the podium."

But someone in the audience insisted, "What about hunting?"

Allegany White Tail Deer

George responded. "In the early thirties the Park was all dirt roads and there weren't any deer. The deer started returning in the late thirties. They brought them in from Michigan and Pennsylvania. They bred them in the Park at Frecks and let a few loose at a time."

George Heron and Friends

Someone else said, "What about Kinzua?"

"We have Removal Day every 5 or 10 years to remind our people of the flooding of Kinzua. It's usually in August. We have a big gathering. We had our first Christmas in Jimersontown in 1965."

"Tell us about Witches' Walk," another called.

"That's where the gold was buried," George responded. "During the Civil War these three Union deserters came by. They met three Indians and gave them a bunch of gold in exchange for some food and clothes. But it was hot money. So the leader of the Indians went back in there, what they call

Witches' Walk, smoking a pipe. When the pipe went out he buried the gold.

"Some people see strange lights back in there they call them Ga-Hi-Neh.

"Old Pete Jackson looked for the gold there all his life. He said, 'Ga-hi my foot. That's the gold shining up through the earth.'"

HOOK FRANCE ON BAY STATE

November 2006

Hook France 2006

About 20 members of the Allegany State Park Historical Society gathered in the Red House museum on November 18, 2006 to listen to Hook (Llewellyn) France tell stories about Bay State. Bay State is the mostly-privately-

owned section of the Park where he was born and still lives. Hook is a 75-year-old retired Allegany State Park Ranger and life-time resident of the Park. For a policeman with the nickname "Hook" he is a friendly, mild-mannered guy. He was dressed in a flannel shirt and leaned casually on a museum case as he talked. He has a prominent sense of humor. He is almost as trim as when he wore a Park Ranger uniform.

Bay State is located in a valley or hollow in the Park and within the township of Red House. It was named after a Massachusetts-based logging company that had been located there. You can reach it by taking a left onto the Bay State Road that parallels Route 86 at the Red House entrance to the Park.

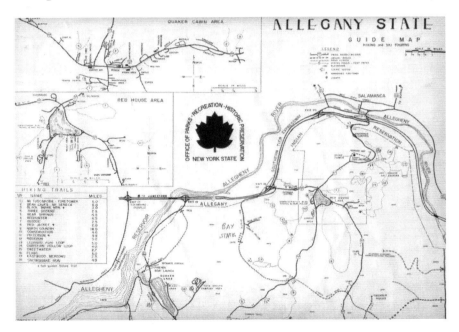

Bay State in red

Here is, roughly, what Hook had to say about Bay State:

"The place was wilderness when the first settlers came. The first one was Darius Frink in 1828. James Rosenberry moved in 1833. In 1849 Marsh and Frisby opened a lumber company there that eventually became the Bay State Lumber Company. There were always about six directors and every three years or so they would go bankrupt and then the same six would start up again with a new name.

"The growth of Bay State was gradual until the Civil War vets came back. A lot of people had gone off to the war. By November 1869 there was enough population to break off from Bucktooth, which was what the town of Salamanca was called then, and form the separate township of Red House.

Jim Carr, in red suspenders, a descendent of Dan Carr's

"On February 23, 1869 they held the first town meeting. Francis Strickland was the first Supervisor. He had his arm shot off in the war. Dan Carr was constable and overseer of the court. The first business was to appropriate $250 for roads and bridges and $100 for the poor. Then they set up a $6000 bond to build a Quaker Bridge across the Allegany. It was to be the same as the one at Hemlock which was what the village of Salamanca was then called. They specified however that the braces were to be made of chestnut and the rest of maple and oak.

"The Bay State Lumber Company haul road was the first road in the hollow. They used horses and wagons to haul logs to the river where they made them into rafts. In the spring the water would come rushing down the river so you could see an actual drop in the water. They would put together a raft and ride it down to Pittsburgh. It'd take three days down and three weeks to walk back.

Cabins at Camp 12

"About Civil War time our family started out at France Brook where Camp 12 is now. My great grandfather left the family in Bucktooth and was gone with his three brothers in the woods for three years building houses and a sawmill at France Brook. They rafted the family and all their furniture down the river to Red House. One of his brothers met them there with a team of oxen and a stone boat to haul them and their furniture up an old lumber road over to France Brook.

"My grandfather got work in the chemical factory at Red House near what is now Exit 19 from Route 86. He moved his family into one of the factory-owned house there. Dad was born up in France Brook. He was six or seven when they moved to the factory house.

"Frank Banks owned the first house you come to on the Bay State Road off the reservation. He had heard about the fortunes to be made in Florida. So he sold his place to my grandfather who moved the family there. Frank packed his family and everything they owned, including a cow, in a box car and moved to Florida. He was back in a year. The best work to be had in Florida was digging potatoes for fifty cents a day.

"Frank went to work in the Bradford oil fields and in a year had four hundred dollars to buy his place back from my grandfather. Then my grandfather bought the Woodmansee place with 50 acres, a house and a barn for $1200. That was our old homestead.

"My grandmother fed the men in the boarding house over in Quaker till 1924. That building is now the Quaker Maintenance Area Paint Shop near Coon Run.

"In 1928 my parents married. I was born in 1931 and my brother, Orville Junior, was born two years earlier. Dad bought the old Burnside house, stable and fifteen acres in Lonkto for us to live in. He tore down a house over in Quaker and used the wood to build two new rooms on to it. In 1940 I remember watching while he had the teams pull those two rooms across the road to start a new house. He used wood from another old house he tore down in Wolf Run to build three more rooms on to it. It was the end of the Depression. No one had any money; you just built with what you had.

"In 1943 Mother and Dad traded that house with my grandparents for the fifty-acre Woodmansee place. Later, when Dad rebuilt the stable into a nice little place for my grandparents, we all wound up living together in the Lonkto house he had built. I was born in Lonkto Hollow, been there all my life except three years in the army.

"One time when I was just a little kid, Dad and Granddad were hauling big rocks out of a field and dumping them into an old cellar. It must have been fifteen foot deep. The bank gave way under one of the horses and he fell in onto the pile of rocks. They quick cut the leather harness so the other horse would not get pulled in. Granddad jumped down in there and sat on the horse's head till they could get the other horse harnessed up to pull him out. They used to do that to keep the horse from banging his head on the rocks. The horse would keep doing that and hurt himself. I didn't know that and I got mad at Grandpa. I threw an orange at him.

Little boy and a team of horses, not Hook but could have been.

Hook had put together a video of his family's homestead sites and he used it to illustrate the next part of his talk. He introduced it saying, "This is no Cecil B. DeMille production. If you don't like it you can have your money back."

The crowd laughed and we sat back to watch the video of Hook in front of a fireplace strumming a guitar and singing:

"There is an old, old house
That once was a mansion"

It showed Hook walking up a dirt road with a sign saying "Beck Road."

On the video, he spoke, "This is back in Lonkto Hollow. In 1928 my father bought a fifteen-acre farm here. Dad built our home there. Three weeks after he died they kicked in the doors, looking for money, I guess."

Hook walked around the wreckage of a little old house painted red. The windows were broken. Hook stepped through the house doorway and said, "I remember when Dad and I poured the concrete for this walk. Every little thing brings up a memory. My grandparents spent their last years here. They moved here to be near Dad.

"We had 15 acres that Dad bought in 1928. I was born here. It was a frame house. The garage was across the way with room for the cow and a tractor. Lonkto Hollow it was called. Now sold to the state. My Great-great-grandmother Stoddard lived up here. I walked a half mile to school. Lot of memories here. Jim Bell lived in a house up the hill.

"There was a big flood that did a lot of this damage. Someone tried to build a fire in here," he said as he walked around in the wreckage past an old fridge and a kitchen table and chair." He pointed to a back room, "I stacked wood in there."

We got to the second section of the video. Hook said, "This was taken a couple years later. This is the road into Bay State Valley. I bought this place, 70 acres, for $18,500."

The video broke down but that did not stop the show. We asked Hook to just go on talking which he did:

"Carl Goodrich married Dad's sister and they had a place in there. Carl always used to get drunk and beat up his wife. One time he was beating on her and Dad pulled him off. Carl went for his gun. Dad got it away from him and threw it away off in the woods. Carl got mad and started punching on him. Dad got him down and got on him, punching. Then Carl's wife, Dad's sister, started clawing at Dad's face and pulling him off Carl, punching him. My grandfather asked Carl, 'Got enough?'

"Carl said, 'No'.

"Grandfather said, 'Ok, give him some more.'

They cut down a lot of big pine trees in there. Used axes because the pitch would bind the saw. Then they figured out to carry along a bucket of kerosene to dissolve the pitch so they could saw.

"George Hubbard worked at the chemical factory. He had a brand new barn built and all set and ready to go for $500. He had his leg shot off at the knee in a hunting accident. When I was a kid their place was deserted. We used to go in there to play around. We found his crutches and a home-made wooden leg there in the barn.

"Hubbard was always fussy about a certain lilac bush. Always shooed kids away from there. Turned out he buried the old leg under that bush.

"In the 1890's old Jim Burnside went off on a rafting trip with a load of logs to Pittsburgh. They sent his pretty young daughter to get a bucket of water. The creeks were running high. She leaned off a bridge; the bucket filled up and pulled her in. They found her up in the willows. She was all buried by the time Jim got back.

"The big girls would play London bridges and they'd haul you off and kiss you or something. That wasn't good for a little guy like me.

"In the 30's the Park hired Dell and Bill Remington to move houses out of land the Park bought up. They got nowhere with it. Then a fellow named Morris from Conawango came down and promised to move out a house a day and he did it.

"He moved Henry Hurdle's homestead. Moved the house first, then the barn. They had to build this great big bridge across the creek with timbers two foot by two foot and forty foot long. Then planks over the top of it. They put 12 by 12 timbers under the barn, then moved it on rollers. He'd drive in stakes and use a 20 part block and tackle so a team could move the barn.

"The house was on one side of the bridge and the barn on the other. One of their horses would never cross the bridge. He'd shy away every time. Then one day he walked across the bridge on his own, looked into the house window and dropped dead.

"Beck Hollow, Phillip Beck lived up in there with his wife Jenny. She had been living with an Indian who had hit her in the head with a hammer. She had a hole in her head. He asked Phillip, 'Would you like a woman?'

"'Phillip said, 'Why yes.'

"'Cost you five dollars.'

"'Ok'

"In the morning she was there with her suitcase and she stayed. Their housekeeping was not too clean in there. When Phillip got done eating he laid his silver on the table and turned his plate upside down until the next meal. I'd go up there with Dad and my mother would always say, 'Now don't you let him eat anything there.' But Jenny always had a sugar cookie for me and it didn't kill me.

Some of the young guys had a stick of dynamite. They always had a stick of dynamite some way. They stuck it on a rock by the Beck outhouse. Jenny came out to use the outhouse and the guys all ran away. I was up at their place next morning at the table with them and Jenny and Phil said nothing.

"Iva Hotchkiss, my first grade teacher, lived near us. Jean Stacey lived next door to them. Once the Stacey's were down visiting us, after supper or something. Someone came in saying there's a big fire down the road. We all piled into our car and it was the Stacey place. Old Al, their dog, had jumped out through a window. The house was ablaze. Jean took an old clothes pole and knocked the wood pile away from the house. At least he saved his wood.

"They stayed with us a month."

Hook has a lot more stories but this seemed like a good point to give him a hardy round of applause and thank him for some well told-tales.

JEFF RUPP
THE SECOND ALLEGANY STATE PARK PATROLMAN

March 2007

Jeff Rupp

Jeff Rupp, a native of Cattaraugus County, comes from Dayton in its Northwest corner. He recently retired after 36 years as a Cattaraugus County DEC Conservation Officer but for six years towards the beginning of his working career he was an Allegany State Park Patrolman. He is also an old friend of Rick Feuz'. When the speaker scheduled for our February 17, 2007 Allegany State Park Historical Society meeting was forced to cancel on short notice, Rick asked Jeff to fill in. Jeff had so many good stories that when he got done we decided that we would have to tap him again to hear about those years with the DEC.

Police Patch Courtesy of Bob Byledbal

He is a slim, sharp-featured man of late middle years with a quick laugh and easy grin. He wore a country outfit, a plaid flannel shirt and dungarees. He called himself a "little guy" but he didn't come across so little to me. Here's what he had to say:

"I grew up in Dayton and Napoli and spent a lot of time in the creeks and swamps up that way; not so much in the big woods like down here. I had no thought of being a cop. My interest was fish and wildlife. After a year at Cornell I wanted a job outside. I took the exam for Park Ranger several years in a row and I scored in the top three but they kept filling the positions with guys from Long Island and way out of town who had seniority. I worked five years in a tannery, looking out the window, asking myself "What am I doing in here?" I was married, had three kids to support and needed a regular check and then I got laid off for two weeks.

"When they formed the Park Police, Park Manager Lee Batterson asked me to join them. I didn't have to think twice about it. But then there was an interval. I got the appointment in the summer and I wasn't to start till December 23. A few days before that the Buffalo News ran a front page picture of an Allegany State Park Patrol Car with a bullet hole through the windshield, put there when they were chasing deer poachers. I came anyway. Paul Bossard was the first Park Patrolman and I was the second.

"It was a kind of a slow start. I came to work on a Thursday. Then we had three days off over Christmas and I came back on a Monday and there wasn't any uniform. It was 1965. The Park was only 44 years old. Now it's almost double the size it was then.

"The first equipment they gave me was a Colt 38 special with a six inch barrel. The holster was on a swivel so when you sat down it changed directions. Several months passed before the uniforms came through.

"Rangers hadn't been police. They were just big men who knew how to twist an arm or kick butt. Then in 1965 they became Police and us new Patrolmen had to go away to school. Rangers never went to school but they gave me on-the-job-training. I went to Red Park's driving school in "AP 1," a black '62 Plymouth 318. You hit a curve and you put the hammer down if you want to catch the bandits.

"The first test I was put to was in that first winter. The kids were in school and we didn't want to take them out to move to the Park until summer. The Park let me take "AP 2" home with me since I had to drive to Mayville to go to Police School. There was a terrible snowstorm and somewhere near Cassadaga I went into a snow drift and down over an embankment. There was old AP 2 with its black butt hanging half way out in the road. I didn't know a thing about a patrol car. I couldn't even operate the radio. Finally a Town truck came and hauled me out.

"Then there was my second big test. I didn't know the Park the way Jim and Hook did. They lived right here. We had those old mud roads, they say lost more mud to wind than to rain. I was in AP 2 down on Route 280. Red Park comes in over the radio "AP 4 to AP 2. What's your location?"

Early Park Police Car
Courtesy of Bob Schmid

"Then I heard the blast of a rifle over toward Wolf Run where the Reservation boundary and the road overlap. Red Park had touched off a round to see how a young buck like me would react to deer poachers.

"I brought my lunch to work in a lunch bucket like a lot of you must have. Once they put a live muskrat in there. Must have got it off the Dam.

"After I finished school I was 'certified' and I could write tickets. The first one I wrote was on a young fellow who was running around all over in his car squeaking the tires on a Saturday night. We used to have Saturday night dances in the Park. People came from all over. The further away they came from the more trouble they wanted to bring. We confiscated a '65 Plymouth station wagon that was half loaded with beer. You had to have a special permit to have beer in the Park. We took those kids up to the dump with us to smash the beer bottles and watch where their money was going.

Park Police Cars 2012

"The Police manned the ski areas. Buster France handled the maintenance. I'd never done any skiing. Red Park was my ski instructor. He took me to the top of the hill and headed me down on my own.
"The Bova area had a rope tow. You had to be careful you didn't get a scarf or gloves grabbed by the rope. Up in Big Basin we had a "Poma" lift. You had to pull down this steel pole with a plastic seat on it and put it between your legs. When you got to the top you had to be sure to get rid of it just

right. Allegany was the "economy" ski place, but we had two ski jumps.

"One Patrolman stood at the bottom of the tow, sold tickets and watched them load on. The other was at the top watching them get off. At the top we had a fire and a warming hut. We were only open weekends. So the mice had the run of the warming hut on weekdays. You couldn't leave any food around. There was an old German couple gave this to me for the hut."

Bova Rope Tow
Courtesy of Bob Schmid

Here Jeff produced an odd device, a screw top glass bottle mouse trap.

" One night I caught two mice in this one trap. The bait was so nice the mice couldn't leave it alone.

"You had to learn to play cribbage up there for some of the slow times."

As he said this, Jeff produced a huge plastic bag from which he extracted a very large, fur-collared, loop-buttoned, khaki storm coat.

"Never saw anyone patrol in one of these things but up at the top of the lift this was pretty comfortable. It's sheepskin lined, weighs ten pounds and is impervious to wind. Who wants to try it on?"

By then Dan Streubel, sun glasses perched on his shaved head, was up in front of the group strutting his stuff in that great relic of a coat.

"When I left the Park Police the supply sergeant didn't want it back so I kept it. He had a kind of a grin on his face when he gave it to me. My wife Diane stored it away. She got it down to bring here and found this ticket in the pocket. It says 'Good for one ride on the Poma.'"

He passed the ticket around for inspection.

"Lee Batterson was the manager when I was here and Mrs. Mooney was his secretary. He was an admirable man, a prince. Asked me to represent him personally to groups that came through down here so I had to study up on stuff."

Jeff has Dan Struebel demonstrate Patrolman's Storm Coat

Here Jeff demonstrated a September 4, 1971 issue of the Buffalo News with a photo of himself and Lee Batterson.

"He had a disciplining method, which he never applied to me. One older fellow he'd give him a can of stain and put him to work staining.

"Parks were part of the DEC till 1970. They say, Governor Rockefeller wanted his brother, Laurence, to run the Parks independent of the DEC but the State Constitution limited the number of regular departments there could be. So he created a Parks Department in the Executive branch of the Government.

"In order to have Rangers in the Park fulltime, the Park gave some of them houses along with an allotment of coal. A couple of them lived up behind the Administration Building and some down on the service road. Hook France and his brother lived in the Park.

"We were living in Dayton 30 miles away. Sometimes I'd work till 2 am and have to drive all the way home. Being the junior man, I drew the short straw on extra details so there was some urgency to live closer to work. That summer we moved into the house across the road from Charlie Dach's restaurant at the Red House ticket booth. That house, I believe, was built to be sold to the Park. The policy was to buy up land in the Park area as soon as it became available. The place had no insulation at all. They had already started to tear it down but Batterson let us have it .We had the furnace red hot all winter trying to stay warm. The next year we found a place in Steamburg and lived there for four years.

"Red House Creek ran behind that Park house of ours and the river. As a kid I was always in the swamp and knew every critter that was there. I had twelve turtles. I painted numbers on their backs and raced them. One time in Red House Creek I saw this round thing. I picked it up. It was soft, rubbery, pliable and had spines. What do you think it was?"

I bit at that one and guessed, "An Allegany Hellbender." I was way off.

"No. It was a Spiny Soft-shelled Turtle, the only one I ever saw.

"The last rattler I saw was from Sunfish around Steamburg. A guy brought him down live. I've never seen a live rattler in the Park. I heard that Wolf Run folks used to make a game of catching them and I heard of some up in Thunder Rock.

"The Park is a special place for me but I loved fish and wildlife so when the chance came up to be a Conservation Officer with the DEC, I took it. I have a kind of spiritual connection with wild things. I have seventeen acres. Now that I'm retired, I spend a lot more time in the woods wondering how to improve the trees, wondering what kids will play there. The trees are my favorite neighbors. Down here in the Park I whisper to them a little. It's just like I never left."

We gave Jeff a good round of applause and then he took a few questions. Bob Schmid asked, "Have you any Black Bear stories?"

Jeff said, "I had a woman take her youngest child up the Bova Dump Road. She got the youngster over next to the bear to take pictures. Could have been some serious incident but there were none while I was in the Park. People do some foolish things.

Black Bear

"Never saw a bear on my own place till recently I saw some tracks. We had open season on bear here lately. Some beekeepers were complaining. We have a humming bird feeder on the porch. This night there was a storm. The thunder and lightning had our Black Lab scared so he was up in bed with us. I heard noise down on the porch. I knew it wasn't the dog. He was with us. It was a bear trying to get the humming bird feeder apart. I called Diane but by the time she got down he was off visiting our neighbor."

Bob asked, "What do you think about the rumor of black panthers around here?"

"I've heard rumors," Jeff answered. "A couple people are adamant about it. I can't say no. Biologists say they could be purchased bob cats or panthers brought here and released. We had a woman once who had a mature lion.

"Keeping wild animals as pets is a problem. A baby raccoon is real cute but a male adult raccoon is down right nasty. Raccoons are the major vector of rabies. If you get bit you have to take that course of shots."

We gave Jeff another round of applause and went up to take turns trying on the storm coat and getting a closer look at that old ticket.

JUDGE LANCE ANDERSON LAW SOUTH OF THE ALLEGANY

May 2008

"How many tickets do they give in Disneyland?" Judge Lance, "Lanny," Anderson asked repeatedly. Judge Anderson serves the Town of Red House, New York, a town now wholly within the boundaries of Allegany State Park. He believes Park operation leans too much toward law and order and too far away from education and recreation. In his court, he tries to rebalance the equation.

Red House Judge Lance Anderson

Before Allegany was a Park, the Judge's grandfather had a farm just south of where the Administration Building is now. The Judge was born in that farmhouse on Anderson Trail, the trail named for his family. His father, David "Dade" Anderson, was a Park Ranger. The Judge himself had a variety of Park jobs including painting cabins. Later he ran a canoe sales business in Salamanca, then took over from long-time Red House Judge June LaCroix. Now, in addition to his judicial work, he travels with NFL Players as a "motivational speaker."

In this session, Judge Anderson wore a white shirt, a black sweater and black slacks. The somber wardrobe fit his dual role of Ordained Minister and Magistrate of the Town of Red House. His speech was earthy and articulate. He had a clear agenda which he conducted from a black leather notebook, reading off topics like "Most frequent or most unusual ticket seen in court."

The Judge controlled the session as he might control a court room using humor and authority and often asking us questions. Bob Schmid tried, once too often, to direct what stories he should cover. The Judge got a laugh out of the audience by telling him, "Bob, you'll have to come up here and tell that story yourself."

The Judge led off with, "The Town of Red House has the smallest population of any town in New York State, 34 as of 2 pm, 37 when my three kids are home from college. It is so small and yet so big. We aren't big enough to poll a jury. If a defendant asks for a jury trial I have to push it up to County Court. We are all cousins, aunts or sisters. I've been a resident for 55 years. Went away to the University of Miami in Florida for a few years. You may ask why I came back from the white sandy beaches of Florida. There is the reason," and he gestured toward a smiling woman in the audience. "There is the reason, my wonderful wife and co-judge, Anne Marie.

"My dad was one of the first Park Cops, along with Sharpie and Lindbergh. They called him 'Dade.' They all rode horses or motorcycles. Dade fell off his motorcycle and he wouldn't ride a horse. He said 'I'll just walk' and he'd walk all the way over to Quaker from Red House. Then they had cars, and story after story about how cars got wrecked running into deer or whatever.

Park Ranger Charlie Lapp and Motorcycle
Courtesy Bob Schmid

"They are no longer Park Rangers. Now they are Park Police. And that was a dramatic change producing a dire effect on recreation in this Park, the third largest State Park in the world. I think Acadia in Maine is the largest.

"Mother Anderson, my mom, came from the notorious Hubbard clan. I drive by where they come from now and just look straight ahead. Never know what they might be up to.

"I've got three kids and two of them are for sale. No, they are good kids. My daughter is at Brockport taking Health

Science. Benjamin is at UB studying English and Cody, the oldest, is our city guy. He is in New York City playing jazz with John Coltrane's son, Ron. It's ironic Cody comes from the smallest town in the state and lives in the largest. Now that's culture shock.

"Red House has the largest per capita number of tickets of any town in the State, 1200 a year. Things have changed. Between 1955 and 65, eighteen defendants requested trials in the Red House Court. That's when the defendant protests and says 'I'm not guilty. Give me a trial.' Now, we do eighteen trials a week. That is because there has been a radical change in law enforcement.

"Under-age drinking, alcohol and speeding are the major causes of the tickets. If I were you, sitting out there in the audience, I would wonder, 'What in hell is going on.'

"How many tickets do they give in Disneyland? Twelve hundred arrests a year in a State Park is a huge number."

Lou Budnick interrupted, "Isn't that because you have the Expressway going through?"

"We get a limited amount of arrests from the Expressway.

"We have four law enforcement agencies in the Park: DEC, Park Police, State Troopers and County Sheriffs. Now, the Park Police are officers and gentleman, yet 1200 arrests is an awful lot of arrests."

Bob Schmid broke in with, "You gotta remember there are 14 Park Police Officers, now."

"There are $75-100,000 in fines plus State, Town and Park surcharges. The Town of Red House has only a mile of highway to maintain and the Town officials are all driving around in brand new trucks. Is that right? You judge.

"I was elected for four years, elected by eight votes. Not eight votes more than anyone, just a total of eight votes. My wife won by eleven. I know who the three were that I lost. They were aunts and cousins where maybe I didn't cut their lawn or something. You might ask, 'How much did I spend campaigning?'"

That got a laugh.

"We are the only husband and wife Judge Team in the State. We combine office and home.

Judges Lance and Marie Anderson

"The most popular tickets are the 600 for under-age consumption of alcohol. Mostly in the spring, from Buffalo. After Prom night there are cabins full of under-21, 16 year-olds.

"And under-age possession of alcohol without being drunk. I struggle with this. You get three guys sitting quietly around a campfire roasting hot dogs, causing no trouble and they're going to have a six-pack of beer standing there. What are you going to do with them?" he asked the audience.

Pete Smallback said "Fine, warn."

Bennett Wheeler said, "Minimum fine, community service."

"They are under 21, but old enough to marry, vote, go shoot people in Iraq. It's a sticky situation. I have to make a judgment and I balance these judgments out with common sense. You can usually tell by looking at them which ones are not horsing around versus a cabin full of kids trashing the place, carving up trees, kicking out railings, smashing windows, up all night partying. I fine those.

"How much of a fine?" he asked us.

Someone said, "Fifteen," someone else, "Fifty."

"Destroying public property is a big one for me. I make them pay restitution. A busted toilet or a sink can cost five hundred to a thousand dollars plus fines. The fine ranges from 250 to 100 apiece depending on the situation. In the Park there is a $15 Park surcharge. You have 20 kids in a cabin each fined a hundred dollars, that's two thousand dollars. And I'll ban them from the Park for one year."

Bennett Wheeler, who is a former supervisor of the Quaker Run half of the Park said, "I used to make them pay for damages on the spot. Empty out their wallets. Sometimes I'd leave them complaining they didn't have enough money to get home."

The Judge said, "Word gets back to Lockport and Cheektowaga High School, 'Don't go to Allegany to party. Go to Letchworth or someplace easy.'"

Lou Budnick said, "What about parents. They ought to be brought in."

"We do that. Parents have to come in and sign," the Judge answered and went on, "Why do they trash bathrooms? Thirty years ago you never heard of that. Are people changing? I think one thing is that these are younger people not used to drinking. A lot of them have two or three beers and go to bed to sleep it off."

I thought the Judge seemed to be missing a point here. A point of which, as an MD, I was painfully aware. I felt compelled to speak up. I raised my hand and said, "If a kid passes out from an alcohol overdose he is very close to dead. How do you deal with that?"

The Judge replied, "A cabin full of drunken kids. What do you do with them? Dump the beer and let them sleep it off? The Park is a laboratory for youth drinking. Safety is an issue the Park has never dealt with. There is a whole bunch of people out there getting hammered. The Court's job is to deal with the tickets."

I pushed it further. "Have you had any deaths?"

"I haven't heard of any deaths in car accidents lately. But this is getting too heavy. You don't want to hear this from me. I'm supposed to make you laugh."

Here Bob Schmid tried again to steer the Judge to what he thought was the Judge's big story. But the Judge just laughed at him and said he'd, "get back to that later."

"Twenty-nine miles an hour in a twenty-five-mile zone around Red House Lake, I have a hard time keeping it down to that myself but they tag 'em for it and it's probably a good thing. It keeps them from going 62. There are dogs and kids on bikes there.

"ATVs in the Park. Only had one. Not much problem with littering. A few dogs off leash. A really big item is Disorderly Conduct, just raising a ruckus. You save six months to bring the kids to the Park for a week and someone keeps you up all night.

He stunned us with this scenario, "Endangering the Welfare of a Child. A twenty-one-year-old guy brings an eighteen-year-old girl to the Park and they are drinking. Technically that's endangering the welfare of a child. What should I do with that?

"Riding in the back of a truck. Depends on the circumstances. I used to do it myself but running around with kids standing up in the back at forty miles an hour with the tail gate down? Three kids got bounced out last year.

"Domestic Violence. She is on the front porch with a butcher knife and screaming. She's gonna' kill him. They've just spent a week in the rain sitting in the cabin staring at each other. And then she put the cooler in the trunk the wrong way.

"We used to go down to Onoville Marina, end of the weekend and watch it. He's in the boat and she's backing up the trailer for the first time. There is screaming and weapons and then they are in court. I hate them. They have to go home separately. They have to have an order of protection to stay fifty yards apart. Then in five or six days they are back in court loving each other.

"Then there is a ticket for shooting a rubber deer. The Park Police have a rubber deer, a big buck with a nice rack and a tail that wags. They put it in the woods 200 feet from the road. It's legal deer season, a hunter comes by in his truck. 'Whoa', he gets out, lays his rifle across the hood and fires away. The Police are behind a big oak a little ways away and tag him for shooting from the road. The guys are so embarrassed. 'Oh my God, I shot a rubber deer.' They have to pay the fine and pay to get the deer repaired."

"Isn't that entrapment?" Lou Budnick asked.

The Judge said, "No one contested it so far. They are too embarrassed.

This is not a Rubber Deer

"Four years ago we had 3-5 DWI's a year. Now we are seeing that many a month. Can anyone guess why?" No one volunteered so he continued, "The Casino. You're playing a machine and they bring drinks over to you. And they charge how much?" He hesitated. "Zippo!"

"Pretty soon you've lost your money and you wind up drunk."

Pete Smallback said "Free drinks? I'm going right over there."

"And I'll see you about 1a.m.," the Judge smiled.

"They take a ride in the Park when they get done. Maybe to sober up or just see the Park. We get a lot of casino activity.

"Life jacket in a canoe. It's a law. You have to have floatation in a canoe. Should you wear a life jacket? We used to have a drowning every year when they rented canoes here in the Park. Those were the main deaths, that and Park dance car smash-ups.

"Feeding the Animals. Years and years people came down to the Park to let the kids feed the animals. Now it is a big ticket item. The cops love giving those. I don't mean feed the kids to the bears," he laughed. Then he added, "There always was a law against feeding animals, but now they enforce it.

"I'm not hard on those tickets. It's a habit, a big thing to ride around the lake and feed marshmallows to the raccoons. In September, after the crowds were gone, I used to pack the family into our conversion van and drive over to the picnic area. The raccoons would be used to being fed and there'd be a mob of them waiting. I'd throw one marshmallow and watch them 'rumble.'

"Most Unusual Ticket. I had a fellow in court. He said, 'It was 3 a.m.. I was in my jammies, slippers and robe. I had to decide to walk or ride to the latrine. I got in the car and all of a sudden I saw the lights flashing behind me in the mirror. The Officer said, 'Do you know why I stopped you? You're not wearing a seat belt.'

"I had another one. Fellow drove across the road from one parking lot to the next over in front of Beehunter. No seat belt. What would you do with that one?

Pete Smallback said "Give 'em a warning.

Bennett Wheeler said, "Fine 'em."

"I'm easy on seat belts. Of course everyone should wear one. But fines are just more dollars for New York.

"Police officers have personalities, like everyone else. Some give warnings, some always give tickets. Some to the extreme. It's not true that they have quotas, but if they never give a ticket I know they have reviews and the Supervisor gets on them. My dad never gave many tickets.

"Every year twenty families get together at one of the group camps for a costume party. Last year they elected me judge. I picked Bob Schmid, dressed up as Bob Schmid, for funniest looking

"I average one wedding a month. I'm ordained so I can do it either way, civil or religious. The most popular spot is the Stone Tower, after that the Covered Bridge, Science Lake and in the cold weather the Ad Building. Quaker Lake Bath House is very popular, too, with the men's room flushing here and the women's over there but they have a pretty view out between the trees and over the water.

"On a personal note from me, the Judge. You may disagree but I have eight voters in my pocket. I am one hundred percent for the reinstatement of Rangers in the Park.

"Rangers were here to educate the public. They'd show you how to build a fire, how to tell dead wood from live. Park Police go to school. Learn how to shoot high-powered rifles. We need a softer approach. There are too many tickets. Again, how many tickets do they give out in Disneyland?

"We need a whole different attitude, a public relations attitude. I have a whole stack of letters on my desk saying 'I'll never come back to the Park, the way I was treated by the Police or the administration.' We need less aggression. Historic preservation, that's how the Park was set up. Park Rangers were 'real' police. Park Police work for the State, not for the Park. There are no quotas, but you write more tickets and there is more revenue.

"So in court I bring it to a balance. How would you handle a ticket for feeding marshmallows to raccoons?"

Bob Schmid said, "Rangers used to talk to you."

The Judge nodded.

Someone else said "Misdemeanor."

The Judge said, "No."

The Judge's answer to himself was circuitous. He started out with a bunch of qualifications and wound up with a kind of parable. I'll try to lay it out close to the way it went:

The Judge took a breath and said, "Well, first of all you should know that Park tickets don't follow you. They don't go on your record. Second, you don't have to pay them. There is no enforcement of paying. And then there is the way things change, even reverse themselves. Marijuana, for example. Thirty years ago, you got caught smoking marijuana you went to jail. Now, it's a twenty dollar fine. And in the other direction, thirty years ago DWI was a slap on the wrist and you went home. Now, you lose your license. A second offense is a felony, mandated by the State.

"People have been coming to the Park to feed animals for years, you can't go cold turkey. You need education. Like the one day I had some ducks to dress out and took them to an Amish lady I know. She took 'em but pointed at a big old goose in her yard and said, 'Look out for him. He'll bite you.' I looked at the goose and laughed. Then he came over and gave me a good hard bite on the back of the leg."

I took the Judge's story in two ways. One, pay attention when they tell you to be careful around animals and two, be careful about your decisions. They may come back to bite you in the butt.

Then the Judge wound things up, "Here's the final story. The one Bob's been wanting. I was a Ranger's son in bed in our place over on Anderson Trail. I heard a gunshot and then another. I looked out the window and there was a spotlight and two deer down.

"Alonzo Sharp and Dade jumped into the old push-button Plymouth Police Car and chased these two guys to the top of Summit. They started shooting at each other. Sharpy said 'I was trying to shoot out their tires.'

"He couldn't shoot and Dade, he couldn't drive.

"The Salamanca Police ran the two guys down on foot along the railroad tracks.

"There were bullet holes all through the Plymouth's windshield but no one got hit. Only Dade and Sharpy could have ducked all those bullets. We called it the 'Showdown at Summit Corral.'"

The Judge left us laughing but also wondering whether he was right that the Park had become too bent on law enforcement instead of on showing people how to have fun in the woods safely. I am sure a lot of folks would agree with the Judge that it would be great to have old time Rangers like "Dade" Anderson, Sharpie and Lindbergh walking the Park again.

JOE OLIVERIO
1940'S ALLEGANY
BAND LEADER

January 2009

Joe Oliverio showed up at our Allegany Historical Society meeting in December 2009 when he heard that Bob was talking. Joe introduced himself briefly as one of the old band leaders from Park dances like the ones Bob was describing. Joe was so entertaining that he threatened to steal the show from Bob and that's not easy to do. So we invited Joe to make his own presentation this month.

Joe Oliverio December 2009

Joe is a smiling, energetic, solidly packed little guy. He's hardly five foot tall but so full of charm that his presence demands your attention. He was dressed in jeans and a new dark blue sport shirt; his gray hair was combed straight back. He wore glasses with oversized lenses fitting his oversized personality.

Joe greeting Bill Wetzel

There was a good crowd that day. Joe had come early and begun talking as he waited eagerly for his turn on stage. But we had a longer-than-usual business meeting which held him back. Then with business taken care of, Bob Schmid decided to introduce Hook France who had not been to a meeting for some time. Hook is a retired Ranger, born in the Park and still living in the Bay State section of the Park. We were all concerned about the collapse of the old Red House Town Hall roof that week, under a heavy load of snow. Bob invited Hook to talk about that building. So Joe had to wait some more.

Hook said, "The old Red House Town Hall used to be out where the lake is now. When they flooded the lake the State moved the Hall to the other side of the dam. I have a lot of memories of that old place. When we had elections, the Democrats sat on one side and the Republicans on the other. One time, Homer Carr ran against John Carr and lost. Homer went up to John in the old Hall and shook a fist in his face. He said, 'You can lick me in the polls but you can't lick me anywhere else.'

Red House Town Hall

"We had Saturday night dances there; the CCC was there. We had weddings, big parties and bands. We played basketball. Red House played against Salamanca. One end was good for shooting, the other end you had to shoot over the stove. The Town Hall was used for everything for a long time. The Allegany Pilgrimage started out there. The Ski Club met there.

"The State repeats itself again and again," Hook declared. "They let a building deteriorate and then they say it has to be torn down. For want of a couple of two by fours and a sheet of plywood, we lost a historic building."

Andy Malicki brought up the loss of the Red House Inn that the Historical Society had hoped to save. Joe was on his feet with, "The Saddle House used to be a great place."

But Rick Feuz restrained him, stepping in to do a formal introduction. Rick said, "Joe Oliverio was a bandleader at the old park dances. Over the phone he kept saying, 'I'm not much of a speaker,' but I couldn't get him off the phone." We all laughed and Joe finally got his chance to talk.

He passed around a framed poster announcing a fifty-cent admission to "Dancing, Round and Square at the Red House Pavilion;" then a photo of the band with him on the trumpet, and last a newspaper clipping of another winter day long ago when there was a ski-jump competition in the Park.

"My parents wanted me to play the violin. When I was eight years old in 1928 they started me with Robert Formica. He came to Salamanca from Milan, Italy to cure his TB. He died of it but he taught me how to play."

Bob Schmid spoke up, "Bob Formica, he played in the Park."

Joe said, "Yes, he played with Dan Carr and he wrote a theme song for Allegany State Park."

Joe went on, "I switched from violin to piano in school. A few years later Lime Lake needed a trumpet. I never played one but I took the job and switched to trumpet.

Joe on the Trumpet

"I had a full scholarship to Saint Boni's but I couldn't finish. My father died and I had to work at the Hotel. We had the Riverview Hotel by the bridge in Salamanca; five floor shows a week."

Here Joe started a spiel as if he were the floor show M.C.: "A girl refused to marry this guy and...he lived happily ever after."

We laughed so he did a longer joke. I got down only a couple of lines. "A guy had a dog named Sex. He went into the Town Hall and said, 'I'd like a license for Sex. The clerk said, 'You don't need a license, just be careful.'" We laughed some more.

"The Hotel is closed now. I was tending bar there once and a guy came in, wanted to sell shares in Holiday Valley Ski Resort. It was Charles Congdon (a founder of Holiday Valley). My dad used to take care of Senator Fancher's horses (Senator Fancher is considered the father of Allegany State Park). He had a spotless barn. Mrs. Fancher had horses in the Park.

"I worked nineteen years on the railroad. Fella told me they had a traveling band. I went in and told the railroad boss that I played the violin. He said you're hired. I played four years. George Willard played with us; he had played with Lawrence Welk. He got his legs cut off in a railroad accident."

I asked Joe, "Outside of the violin, what was your railroad job?"

"Car repair and inspector; I tested air brakes. I was on the tap-rivet gang, did welding and worked as a carpenter." His eyes lit up, "The grain used to get behind the car lining. We would pick it up and sell it. We got two dollars a bag. We'd get five or six bags out of a car.

Joe said, "I was out of work at the railroad from June to October, drawing unemployment. Charlie Dach hired me to play for dances in Red House on Friday and Saturday. On Sunday we'd play in Quaker. I played the violin for square dances; worked with Gus and Leo Remington and Dan Carr. Terry Parks from Logan was the last of them. They've all passed away. We had good crowds. The parking lot was full and cars lined the roads. It was 1945 and 46. There were no jobs. The Park was their playground. Fenter Village Amusement Park was operating at the Summit entrance. They had big bands.

Quaker Dance Hall just before demolition

"I got laid off from the railroad and Dales Brothers Circus hired me to play in their band. We toured the South and Midwest. They paid as good as the railroad and the food was terrific. I met many Ringling Brothers performers and got to Hollywood. I even led the Lawrence Welk band in one number.

"Someone asked me how I got into harness racing. Well, I thought if I bought a horse and went to the track I'd get some good tips and win money. I did make it into a national magazine once when I won $80 on a $2 bet. I owned horses; put shoes on them, drove them. Finally one freezing cold morning when I was 70 years old, I asked myself what am I doing out here jogging a horse.

"I'm a licensed stock broker. I was working for the railroad. The brokerage wanted me to come full time. I made more money on the stock market than on my job.

"My grandson, Anton, is one of the top six drummers in the United States. When he was twelve, he came in second in a national drum competition, with adults. He should have won the finals in Hollywood. First prize was a car. They couldn't give a car to a twelve-year-old. He was featured in the June 2006 issue of Drum magazine. They asked him, 'What is your ambition?' He told them, 'To have a dressing room with an unlimited supply of pizza and Sprite.'

Dan Oliverio played with Iron Horse Hendry and Big Wheely and the Hub Caps at Red House Dances
Photo courtesy of Bob Byledbal

"A couple years ago they came down and asked me to play taps at the Salamanca High School Alumni dinner. I hadn't touched the horn in years; didn't even know if I could find it. I found it but could hardly blow it. I been playing taps for the Alumni dinner ever since."

Joe paused, then started with, "I worked 19 years on the railroad…" His wife, judging that time was up, said, "And you haven't done nothing since."

Rick Feuz got up with a plaque he had made to mark the occasion, "Before you two break-up, I better give you this and say 'Thanks, Joe, you were great.'" We all applauded.

JOHN "JUMBO" FELLOWS

April 2008

The sun shone bright and 87 degrees warm in Allegany that third Saturday in April. The Park was unusually full of people outdoors. Still we had a good crowd in the Administration Building because "Jumbo" Fellows was coming to talk and he had a reputation as an authentic Allegany Personality.

Rick Feuz left and Jumbo Fellows right

Folks were finishing their cake and coffee and finding seats in the Great Room. Rick Feuz rose and started his introduction, "John 'Jumbo' Fellows was a Road Engineer in this area for many years," as this friendly giant made his gradual progression through an audience containing many of his old friends. Jumbo shifted his cane from right to left hand to stop and shake with old Seneca Nation President, George Heron. Jumbo touched the peak of his US Navy baseball cap and nodded to Allegany State Park Commissioner Laurie Peterson and then grinned and shook hands with her husband.

Jumbo greeting an old friend

Rick continued, "He was only five to seven years old in 1934 when his mother got the job as CCC nurse in the Park. She had the office above the Police at the far end of the Administration Building." Jumbo was towering above Rick at that point, smiling and shaking hands with him. Rick added, "I promised Jumbo, you'd have lots of questions for him."

Jumbo turned to the audience, "Hope you don't mind, I can't stand only so long and I can only sit so long, too. So if I fall over you can just let me be.

"When I first came here I was only seven years old. The Park was in its infancy. My mother, Nellie Fellows, was introduced to Mister Roosevelt (President Roosevelt) and he got her this job as CCC Nurse. At the time, Mister Smith was the Administration Building Janitor. He had an apartment where the Police are located now and we had the apartment over his. The Police were located at the other end of the building and her office was upstairs over them. I was told, 'Never to interfere with the CCC.'

Jim and John Fellows, John handling Hawk

"After that first year, I was only allowed in the Park on weekends because of school and I would get a ride from the River View Hotel. Two girls who had a car picked me up there and got me here. In the summer it was harder.

That first year I was kind of randy I guess and I was told to report to Mister Lindberg (Oscar Lindberg), the Chief of Park Police. For punishment, he assigned me to work for Bert (Egbert Pfeiffer the curator of the ASP outdoor Zoo) in the Petting Zoo. You all know where that was, on the hill right behind here." With his cane, Jumbo pointed out the door and up the hill behind the Administration Building.

He picked up a photo off the table at the front of the room and passed it around. "I'm the good looking one on the right," he said. The photo showed him and another smaller boy standing in the zoo. Jumbo, age seven, was holding a good-sized hawk on his right arm.

Zoo Bear Cubs Soot and Smoke
Courtesy of Bob Schmid

"Bert trained me to handle hawks. He'd take me with him when we went off to various camps to put on demonstrations. He'd take me along, too, when he had to go out and catch raccoons and rabbits for the zoo. But not if he was going after something dangerous like a rattler. Or a bear. Oh no, nothing like 'Sonny you go in there and let the bear follow you.' No, nothing like that," he said with a grin.

"He'd leave me and I'd stay behind cleaning cages. I had to move the eagle to another cage while I cleaned his. It wasn't easy. That eagle was just about as big as me. Had to clean the deer cages, too. I'd move them up front for people to see while I cleaned the back cages and then I'd move 'em back again.

"Bert would tell me "Put peanuts in there and get some worms for over there. Back up the path towards Kings Row (the five houses that are located behind the Red House Administration Building) we had a hole. I'd take the waste from the animal cages up there in a wheelbarrow.

"He showed me how to make a canoe out of birch bark, small one, to make into a flower box.

"Before I met him I didn't know anything about animals. If I saw a rabbit I'd hit it with a stick.

"He never earned much money. If he made $30 a month he was lucky. Sold the canoes.

"Then I went to work summers, when I wasn't in school and didn't get here so much but I always made Memorial Day. Then I was away for a time during the War. And ever since, we always come down here for picnics and to stay two weeks in the summer.

"In 1946 over by the lake, they had a dance hall and grocery store run by Charlie Biddell. Me and a couple of buddies would sleep there. Rich folks, we called 'em, would come down from Buffalo on weekends. We'd hang around them with sad faces, worse then Yogi Bear, when they were cooking. They'd feed us nice big juicy hamburgers instead of a dried up old hot dog or something from the store. Charlie Jann, Delores Eckenrode, we were all good moochers.

"On the Quaker side, if you went to the right, there was Mooney's Bar Room (Mooney's Tavern located in the Town of Quaker Bridge) and to the left was Scriptors (Quaker Bridge Fairmont Creamery) for ice cream. It was really a milk factory but we went there for their ice cream. That's where the school teachers had their cabins away from the kids for a change. There was a grocery store (Bob Banks Trading Post) and a five-house community (Buzzardville). Camp Turner used to be on the right, now it's on the left. Then the Ad building and across the way, behind the food store, there was the Quaker Dance Hall.

"My wife and I used to like to get one of those riverside cabins (Angle Trail). Sit on the porch and watch our kids over in the pool, we had an agreement with the lifeguard. If he had to blow his whistle at any of them all four were sent home for the day.

Second Fancher Pool
Courtesy of Bob Schmid

Jumbo paused. Someone in the audience took advantage of it, "Where was the closest saw mill?"

Jumbo thought for a moment, "Between here and Red House, there was a lumber company and a chemical company.

Chemical company is not the proper name for it though…" he let the thought drop. "Ten years ago you could still see the foundations. Near the CCC camp. Robert Lee was the cook there. Later on he ran a lunch room alongside the theater at the bridge in Salamanca."

The questioner said "I heard of a saw mill somewhere on top of a mountain here and I was puzzled."

That puzzled Jumbo as well.

But Jim Carr raised his hand and volunteered, "In the 30's and 40's there was a lumber mill up English Brook Road a ways. And in '46 one by the C's camp."

A Fellows Family Reunion

Lou Budnick, sitting in the front row, asked "Do you recall the Buffalo Museum of Science Camp?"

"Mostly girls," came Jumbo's quick reply that got a laugh. "Of course I was only seven years old at the time.

"We'd show our eagle over there. Bert would have the eagle and I'd be running around with a hunk of meat. Coming after it, the eagle would almost knock me over."

Someone else asked, "Did the CCC sustain many injuries? How did your mother treat them and where would they go if they were seriously hurt?"

"She wouldn't tell me stuff like that. She'd tell me, 'Go feed the chipmunks or something.' I guess if they were hurt bad they'd take 'em to Salamanca District Hospital"

"Did the Park have a fire department?"

"No."

"Who did the stone work in the Park?"

"I think that was mostly the CCC."

Janet Pfhol asked "Do you know anything about Irish Brook, the families that lived there?"

"No. Ask my daughter, she's the genealogist."

Jumbo Saying Hello to George Heron

Jim Carr broke in, "The stone work was a mix. CCC did some of it. My grandfather, Henry Carr, did a lot. John Sikora, he was a stone mason, he did a lot, too."

Jumbo smiled, "John was a big man and he was strong. Came into the Bar Room once, said he could pick me up and he did, bar stool and all."

George Heron broke in from his bench in the back of the room alongside his son. "Jumbo's father was Salamanca Chief of Police. He was a little bit bigger than this Jumbo" and he paused for a laugh.

"Don't know many people know it anymore but Jumbo's father was famous for putting a drunk in a cab and he'd pay his fare home."

Jumbo responded. "Some of them would come by canoe. They'd walk steady to the canoe coming but pretty wobbly getting in it on the way back."

"Any bear stories?" came a cry from the rear.

Jumbo took it up, "Two years ago a bear was raising heck. There was a guy out there with a camera backing away. He thought the flash would stop the bear but he kept coming at the guy and then shot on by. The guy showed me the picture. Bear had the whole side of his head raw. I said, 'Show it to the Rangers.' And darned if they didn't put a big noisy trap right in front of my trailer.

"The bear burned himself digging garbage out of a fire.

"Then another time. Noise woke me up. There were fifty people out there coaxing a bear. You don't coax a bear. Don't do that night or day.

"My daughter's son had just been bit by a rabid fox. My grandson comes running in 'Bear, Bear.' We go out there and there is this guy with a camera telling his little guy 'Pet him. Go ahead pet him. I'll get your picture.' I told him. 'A bear's a wild animal. You run out of food and he'll eat you'."

"How about snakes?" someone asked.

"In the zoo the dangerous snakes were kept in glass cages where the glass curved in so if you did reach in he couldn't get you. There were rattlesnakes over in Wolf Run."

Andy Malicki, sitting up front by the windows, asked about Park roads.

"Bay State Road was the main road and France Brook was used. The one from Quaker was the way to Bradford. The ladies would still all come in long dresses and bonnets when I was a kid. And they had Studebakers, long cars. Blue collars had Fords. The rest of the rich folks had Buicks and Cadillacs.

"I bought a big old Buick after the war for $50. It had three seats in it and huge headlights. We were driving it around in the Park, came over the hill and there was a cop on a horse. Pretty soon three police cars were chasing us. Who ever heard of putting a license on one of those old junk cars? You just bought an old car for $10, run it till it died. Well, that one costs me $30 in court and $30 was hard come by in those days."

George Heron was listening close. He laughed and said "Jumbo and I used to work together. He was Operating Engineer on the Expressway...so he didn't have much to do. Remember he'd be sitting in the bar with a bottle of Genny."

"Now, now, don't be telling tales," Jumbo said, laughing and speaking over George. "I used to, but after I retired in 1978, I haven't had a drop since. I used to drink a case a day, for years and years; six pack on the way to work, six pack at lunch, six pack on the way home and six pack in the evening. I quit drinking and I got sick. I never was sick till I stopped drinking. That's what brought all this on," and he waved his cane in explanation. "I tell you, if you ever get into drinking heavy, don't stop quick. Do it little by little."

The crowd showed its pleasure with chuckles and applause. Rick Feuz stepped forward and closed the session by presenting Jumbo with a carved wooden plaque showing a mischievous urchin with a large hawk on his shoulder. Jumbo accepted it with a grin and worked his way back through the crowd, chatting and shaking hands.

PART TWO

PASSIONS

HOT DOGS AND MARATHON SKIING

February 2005

It was a gorgeous day for a cross country ski marathon—crisp temperatures and blue skies. New snow covered Allegany State Park's world –class cross-country ski area . The wonderful smell of sizzling hot dogs lingered in the air.

Summit Warming Hut

It was the Art Roscoe Ski-a-thon. Art, a Park forester, laid out the ski area at the top of the hill where you come in from Salamanca. His trails follow old logging railroad grades with panoramic vistas through the hilltop forest. They are ideal for my brand of ski-ambling and for racing, too.

Summit Fire Tower

An abandoned fire tower that we are restoring sits in the midst of the ski area. Race organizers offered to share proceeds with the tower committee for feeding the racers. I went to the event just to cook hot dogs. But the spirit of the athletes in flashy Lycra suits waxing skis and charging down trails, swept me away.

Our charcoal fires were burning well and no one wanted to eat hot dogs at 9:30 a.m. So I strapped on my skis to show off my stuff on the Sweetwater five-kilometer course.

Well Dressed Racer

The start of the course is uphill. I was moving smoothly. Then, behind me, came an unfamiliar slap, slap, slapping. If my skis make any noise it is a swoosh, swoosh. But this fellow was putting so much into it that the tail of his skis rose off the snow and slapped back down with each lunge. I went into second gear, tried slapping mine down and stayed ahead until politeness overcame me. I was not registered to race and he was into serious preparation. I stepped aside. He shot past and my grateful cardio-respiratory system attempted to recover.

Of course he is using waxable skis, I thought. If I had been waxing, it might have been different. To wax, you apply a sticky wax at the mid-point of the ski, under your boot, and glide wax fore and aft. It's fast but you have to get it just right and I never had.

I started a half hour before the race, figuring that was time enough to round the course and be out of the way. I did not anticipate superhuman velocity. I moved on enjoying the view and listening to a chickadee here and there. The temperature was in the high teens. I grew warm under my fleece and parka. Reasoning that you wear out quicker if you sweat too much, I took the time to strip off a layer.

In the Warming Hut

Slap, slap, slap, a flash of skintight black Lycra shot by me. There was brief silence and, in a blaze of scarlet and indigo, the second-place racer bulleted by. I dodged aside expecting an onslaught but these guys must have been Olympians. No one else was close. Their sleek appearance turned me to an inventory of my own baggy blue-gray outfit. Of course they're fast. They've got the right wardrobe.

I attacked the trail with renewed determination. Then, with such a slapping, grunting and swooshing like I had never heard, the pack zoomed in on me.

"On your right." "Thanks." "On your right." "Thanks," they called. I took the hint and quickly moved to one side.

Courtesy took its toll on my speed –such as it was. I had had enough of this high speed stuff. Dripping sweat, I skied back to the refreshments. All the cooking jobs were filled. So I smothered a hot dog with chili from a steaming bucket and gobbled it down.

The Cooks

The crowd of watchers saw rapture cross my face as, dripping chili and sweet onions, I inhaled another. They joined in. So now I know where I fit in best at a ski marathon. I was the perfect shill, for the hot dog stand.

ALLEGANY CHRISTMAS STORIES

December 2006

'Twas a couple weeks before Christmas
But we didn't care
That Saint Nick wasn't there
We partied anyway

Christmas Bob Schmid and Chris Babcock 2006

All the heat was off in the Red House Administration Building so fires were set blazing in the fireplaces at either end of the Great Room. A ten-foot balsam Christmas tree decorated the French window bay and big black cut-out bears were set there sniffing piles of tempting wrapped boxes. We had had our brief Allegany State Park Historical Society meeting and election of officers. Regional Director Mike Miecznikowski dropped in to wish us a Merry Christmas. We gave outgoing-President Andy Malicki a special edition Allegany 75th Anniversary Zippo lighter for his dedicated efforts over the last few years. And I won the raffle of a wooden plaque Rick Feuz had carved. The plaque dramatically displayed a great big Allegany bear which kind of set the tone for the rest of the day.

Historical Society Gathering in the Great Room

So then we got to the real Christmas business of eating and telling stories. Two long tables were stacked with cakes, cookies, candy, deviled eggs, sausages, nuts, pizza and wings.

We stuffed ourselves and, still nibbling, formed a story-telling circle in front of the fireplace nearest the food.

Well, it didn't happen exactly like that. I had to prod them a little to get the stories going. Here are a few of them as close as I can recall. Excuse me if I remember my own a little better than everyone else's but you can correct that by being the scribe at next year's party.

Tom Quinlan spins a Tale

A woman, a poor stranger, who had come for a walk in the Park and stumbled on our party, began the story-telling. She wasn't familiar enough with our situation to know that most of us were too embarrassed to start off so she got right into it. "I was hiking here a while ago and I was admiring the covered bridge. A couple there saw me looking at the stone work. They showed me an almost perfect butterfly in the stone pattern. You know how it is. A couple of young guys bored with just laying up stone found two, almost matching, big colorful rocks that made a perfect pair of wings. It's beautiful. I was over there looking at it today."

Tom Quinlan, not to be outdone by a newcomer, stepped forward with, "If you look out by the flagpole." And he gestured toward the front of the building. "In the concrete at the base someone inscribed 1975. While it was still wet someone else rushed down there with a little baby and put both of the baby's feet in the concrete. You can see the two deep little prints there."

The Campbell Family and (right) Alice Altenburg

The Campbell family was present in force, two couples. They had come laden with cakes and I think they brought the éclairs too. Bob Campbell was on his feet before Tom was done. "My brother and I were born in the Park over in Quaker Bridge. Roland Remington and his family lived down there, too. We had the big barn there. Every winter they cut up ice out of the pond and stored it in there in sawdust. One time we had a party there with a big spread of food laid out and a bear came up and scared everyone away."

His wife Anita said, "We went to school in that one-room school house; it's a cabin on Holt Run now. But what we'd always do when we came to the Park was drive up to the dump to see the bears."

Bob Schmid's ears perked up at the mention of bears and he swooped up in front of the fireplace for a better command of the audience. Laughing, he said "I don't want to offend Larry there. I know how he feels about bears. But I remember my Dad one time. He had a basin full of food and he was tossing it out at this great big monster of a bear. The bear was eating it up as fast as Dad could throw it out and the bear was catching up to Dad. Dad kept backing away till he was up the stairs and inside the cabin door. I can remember that big old bear standing with a giant paw on either side of the door looking in on us. It's a wonder he didn't come on in."

Trying to throw Bob off the scent, I picked up on Roly Remington, "He once told me about the milk house they had on their farm over in Quaker. A stream ran right through the milk house and inside they had a concrete cooling tank for milk cans. When he was a kid, he used to catch trout and put them in the tank. Then when city kids would come down he'd take the kids in there. They'd poke their fingers in the water and get bit by the trout."

That got a pretty good laugh and Lou Budnick came in with, "Did you ever fish for crayfish? My grandfather used to love to eat crayfish and we'd catch them to take home to him. One time I caught this big bottle full of them and left them outside of our cabin over night. In the morning they were all gone."

"Raccoons got them," someone piped up.

Lou went on, "So next day we filled up the bottle with crayfish again but this time we put great big heavy rocks on top of it. During the night there was a big racket out there, the bottle smashed and they were gone again."

Someone asked if you could eat crayfish. Grace Christy answered, "That's OK. You can eat them. Just make sure the stream they come from isn't polluted."

Then I remembered catching crabs, that's what we called them, "crabs." "We used to stay on Ryan Trail. There is a little stream that runs behind the cabins and we caught lots of crabs in there. Then my cousin Bobby came down and I took him wading out in the crick to catch some. I had a mayonnaise jar in one hand and I lost my balance. I swung my arm around to catch myself and smashed the bottle right on his head. Bobby never developed the attachment to Allegany that I have."

Meghan Schmid tells her Story

Tall, raven-haired, sixteen-year-old Meghan Schmid was hanging back a little but her Dad called on her. It looked like she'd been rehearsing for this. "When I was little," she said, "I first learned to ride a bike in the Park. I wanted to keep up with the big kids and they were all jumping off this porch. So I got up there and jumped, too. Only there was this iron spike. I landed on it and got cut. So all in the same trip I had my first bike ride and first stitches."

Recently-wed Chris and Julie Babcock sat together on a couch close to the fire. He volunteered. "The first time I came to the Park I was probably a fetus." Nobody said it but it raised the question: might there be another very young Babcock visiting the Park at that very moment?

Bob Campbell talked about his 93-year-old dad who wanted to be here today but got tied up in something else. "He is full of old stories about the Park. He was working once planting pines near the Quaker entrance and someone remarked to him. 'Well, we'll never see these grown up.' They are grown very tall and Dad is still admiring them.

Bob Schmid took the floor again and said, "On kind of a sad note, you probably remember Old George. He was a great big bear, probably easy went 700 pounds. And the thing about him was he had this great big head." Here Bob indicated the size of the behemoth's head, making a three-foot-in-diameter hoop with his arms. "Old George got run into by a semi down on the highway just a few months ago. It was real sad. Everyone liked to see Old George."

There was quiet and a smattering of questions about the circumstances.

Then Meghan broke the lapse with, "I used to like to go ride with my dad and the men at night to spotlight animals. This one time my mom and the other women didn't want to go. They stayed at the campfire. We were out in the car looking and looking and looking and didn't see anything. We came back to the campfire and found out that's where we should have stayed. The women had seen a bear and all kinds of animals."

Tom raised a hand and said, "That reminds me. My family, every year we rent Camp 12 for a week and sometimes it's kind of annoying having people drive by shining spotlights into camp at us looking for animals. So this uncle of mine made a couple of big black bear cut outs. We put them up out there in the field by the road. Was kind of fun to see the lights go by and then stop; do a double take and go back. The second year we tried a moose and an elk. This year we are going to do circus animals, a giraffe and maybe a gorilla."

That got a few belly laughs. So I said, "Speaking of animal hoaxes, I remember one of these Christmas story sessions a couple years ago. We were up in the dining room and someone pointed to the moose head up on the wall. He said, 'You know when I was a kid my dad had me fooled. He said if we could get around to the other side of that wall we could see the whole moose. And I believed him for years.'"

I enjoyed the reaction that got from the crowd but soon felt guilty about it. Andy, who had been pretty quiet, spoke up, "That was me. It was the deer head on one end of a kind of a box in the wall and my dad said the rest of the deer was inside."

I tried to recoup the situation with this one, "Back in 1937 my sister and I came to summer camp at Camp 12. It was the Turnverein Camp in those days. One night we were all sitting on the ground around a big campfire outside the dining hall. We were singing songs and listening to stories when this really big bear came into camp and tore the door off our garbage shed. The shed was only from here to that wall away from us."

My audience gasped appreciatively. I went on. "The next day or so I was alone for some reason in the middle of the day, maybe skipping out on nature study or something, and the bear came walking back through camp. Used to be a row of cabins to the north of the dining hall and the bear was going right down the road between them. He looked kind of fuzzy and nice so I wanted to pet him. I followed him along trying to catch up. Then he turned and stood up on his hind legs with his mouth wide open and these great big teeth showing. But he was holding out one paw. I went to shake hands with him and..."

Rick Feuz Supplied the Bear

"Oh no! You, Larry Beahan?" Bob exclaimed.

I said, "Yes, I thought maybe he was smiling."

Again the crowd gasped or at least I'd like to think they did and someone said "And?"

I said, "I misjudged him. He ate me right up. I was never heard from again."

They laughed pretty well at that one and I think it's a pretty good place to wind up this thing.

So Merry Christmas. See you all next year. And don't be a Teddy Bear's picnic.

ALLEGANY HOOTENANNY
SALLY MARSH

Sept 2008

Sally Marsh is a beautiful bounding ball of laughter, joy, song and love. She has been wowing them at her Thursday night Hootenanny in Quaker Run amphitheater for thirty-seven years. And this rambunctious lady wowed our crowd, too, telling her passionate story. She had us Allegany Historical Society fuddy-duddies crooning "King of the Road" and shouting the "Dingaling" song.

Sally Marsh and the Budnicks at St. John's-in-the-Woods

In her red, white and blue Stars-and-Stripes T-shirt, curly blond hair flying; with her great big smile shining; all in constant motion, I had to think of her as the campfire bouncing-ball, like the ones in the old movie sing-a-longs but a lot prettier and sexier.

The Cover of Sally's raucous Songbook

Sally began her Thursday night summertime Hootenanny sing-a-longs in the Park when she was seventeen.

"When I was little," she said, "my mother worked in the Ad Building. Everyone loved her. They had to. She was the payroll clerk and handled all the medical benefits. I knew all the Park Police and they'd give me a ride over to the Quaker pool every day. They are all gone now. I was always a good swimmer and so I got hired as a lifeguard, the first girl lifeguard in the New York State Park system.

Quaker Amphitheater Stage

"The guy in charge of Quaker knew I had a guitar and could sing. He said "How about a sing-a-long. The Amphitheater was just a hill then, with logs for seats. Forty people showed up. We had a fire. The first ten years there was no pay. But hundreds of people started to come. I made these songbooks." Sally was already bouncing on and off the little stage and moving up and down the aisle at Saint John's-in-the-

Woods Chapel. She gave us all copies of her songbook. "These have traveled 'round the world," she said.

"After while, we had electric guitars. Now we've got Karaoke.

"I used to come around with a portable mike with five extension cords patched together. I'd get people to sing over the mike. Couples would have to get closer together to sing. Now I've got a cordless mike. There is no place you can hide. I can chase you down in the outhouse.

Sally Marsh in Action

"I've been writing a book. I've got hundreds of stories." Here Sally choked up for a moment. I could see her tears. "A guy just back from Iraq came up to me on a Thursday night. He said, 'Over there, all I could think of was, I want to get home and go to one more Hootenanny. That's why I'm here tonight.

"There was a little kid waiting for heart surgery, all he wanted was one more Hootenanny

"A fifty-year-old couple met here in the Park when I made them sit close to each other and sing. They came on their anniversary.

"The singing Scinta family came every summer and sang along. I've been out to Las Vegas and hailed them up on the stage. "I'm here; it's Sally from Allegany.'

"I've got eight kids. They all come here for summer vacation and sing with me."

"There was a time we brought a piano over from Camp Turner. We should have tried it out. It was all frozen up and wouldn't play.

"I worked my way through college with jobs here in the Park. Did everything from garbage to rental office and toll booths. Alone out in no-mans-land at the Bradford entrance I'd practice my guitar. Then I taught phys-ed in high school, used a lot of music there. I retired at 51. People get mad, I got to retire so young.

"Now, every Thursday, four or five hundred people come out to the Hootenanny. They're dancing and singing, meeting old friends, having fun and good times. It's such a cool thing. People come from all over. Teenagers drive in from Salamanca. Old folks and young hug each other. Little kids get up and sing *Leavin' on a Jet Plane*. People want the old songs. At the end, we all hold hands and sing *God Bless America*. What a patriotic moment that is.

"The first ten years we never got paid. After that we got paid off and on. Mike Miecznikowski was Park Manager then. He sent me a letter, 'Sorry we have to shut down. I can't pay you.'

"I told him, 'Mike, you think I do it for the $50.00?' Just schedule it for Thursday nights. I don't even need the money.

"There's some lady in Albany that keeps cutting the pay and the number of weeks I'm on the schedule. Folks got a petition together, 1870 signatures. People wrote letters like, 'I was at Allegany and there was no Hootenanny our week. How come?' or 'Why no Hootenanny on the Fourth of July.' Six thousand letters.

"The State Parks Commissioner Castro called me from Albany and apologized and put me back on the schedule. Thirty-seven years I've been doing the Hootenanny now and I only missed three times and that's when I was in the hospital. The time with my appendix I told my mom if I could just get there for a little while. So if I don't show up you know I'm in the hospital.

"One time they printed the schedule wrong. We got to the Amphitheater at eight. There were four hundred people waiting. They'd been there since seven. What a cheer they gave us when we walked in.

Sally took a breath and Lou Budnick shouted a question from his second row seat. "How do you get kids, who are addicted to Ipods and video games, to sing?"

"It's no problem. Singing is a fun thing that they don't know about. I show them and they get right into it."

Then Rick Feuz called from the back, "Don't you get a power rush when you are standing up leading that gigantic crowd?"

Sally answered, "No. There's no power in it. Some say I could get the Pope to sing Country. It's just happiness. Don't even care if I don't get to sing, as long as I can get the crowd to sing."

I asked Sally, "Have you had bears try to get into the act?"

She answered laughing, "Oh yeah, bears and raccoons. After the show in the dark we asked one girl, 'Do you want a ride home.'

"She said, 'Oh no, I'm alright.'

"Just then a bear walked by, 'Yup, I'll take it.'

"I saw a couple put a blanket down in a nice private spot way at the back of the Amphitheater. While I was watching, a bear walked behind them. They got up real quick and moved into the crowd.

"The weather always cooperates. It can be raining everywhere. It certainly rains at Allegany. But never on Thursday between 7 and 9 in the Park; you can count on it. If it looks like it might rain, we sing *Raindrops Keep Falling on My Head* and that stops it.

Rick Feuz awarding Sally one of his "Country Carvings"

She said kind of regretfully, "We used to have a fire. Great fires. The kids would spend a week collecting wood and building it. Someone would tend it during the singing. Safety problem I guess.

"We never have trouble. Oh, the police cruise by and have a look but never any problems. Once a kid threw a fire cracker. Two big guys got up and went over to sit on either side of him.

"Let's sing some songs," she said, waving her copy of the Hootenanny songbook... What do you want to sing?"

My wife, Lyn, had found her favorite in that book so she shouted "King of the Road." We clicked our fingers and sang our way through that delightful syncopated oldie. Sally made a point of making us two old smoochers sort of cuddle while we sang and she wound up telling me, "See, wasn't she impressed?"

Sally had the crowd laughing, shouting out the Dingaling song and a bunch of others from her Hootenanny songbook. Finally breathless she said "Thanks and so long," while we were all still high on song. As we applauded, she was into the crowd. About half of us got a bear hug from her before she was done.

ALLEGANY SKI JUMPING
TED LA CROIX

April 2006

Allegany Jumper in Flight
Photo Courtesy of Bob Schmid

The Red House Ski jumps were used in national competitions from the '30s to the '70s. There was downhill skiing, serviced by lifts from the '40's through the 80's, first at Bova in Red House and later in the Big Basin. Skiing in Allegany State Park now is primarily done in the Art Roscoe Cross-country Ski Area in Red House.

Ted La Croix 2006

Ted LaCroix burst into our meeting in the Red House Administration Building lobby, excited, full of energy and loaded with souvenirs of his youth. He was born in Allegany State Park and grew up to be a ski champion here. The souvenirs he brought were for our Historical Society collection; 1960's Head skis and leather boots, a trunk full of ski medals and trophies and two ancient Allegany State Park fire fighting rakes.

Some of Ted's Trophies

Ted is in his middle sixties but looks younger, slim and trim in jeans, cowboy boots and a Stetson. He just retired from running the restaurants at Ellicottville's Holiday Valley. His dad worked thirty years for Allegany State Park. His mother, after waitressing for Charlie Dach in the Administration Building and at the Red House Inn, became Red House Justice of the Peace for many years.

Standing before the Historical Society he said, "It was a great privilege to grow up in the Park." Then he took a breath, "I know I'm supposed to talk about ski jumping but I may wander a bit. If I talked ski jumping as long as I jumped, I might be up here kind of short."

"I started skiing when I was four with a pair that had little leather straps for over your toes. We lived in one of that row of houses below the dam right across from the jumps. The houses were moved there from where the lake is now. The old one-room schoolhouse there burned down and was rebuilt. I went to the new one from first to sixth grade. Later it was the home of our Inter State Ski Club.

"We used to go to school in our ski clothes and do a 30-meter jump at lunch. Darwin Boyer was one of the best jumpers that came out of the Park. He had a construction company. One time he built us a skate pond three feet deep by the club house. We ran a fire hose into it from the crick across the road. When we went out to check it at 3 am, all the water was in the ditch. It leaked like a sieve.

"My Grampa Fuller's barn was where the old Town Hall is now. There are a lot of stories about that place. Lee Remington used to call square dances in the Town Hall with a pipe sticking out of the side of his mouth. One time when George France was Town Constable, Red House had a tied vote in an election. He had to occupy the Town Hall for three days. He slept with a shotgun alongside his cot.

"Grampa Fuller's sugar bush became Sugarbush Trail. I made a lot of sugar there.

Ski Jumps, 2011

"In the early 1930s, they built the jumps right across the way from the schoolhouse. Karl Farner designed them. They were 30 and 50-meter jumps, should have been 40 and

60. Jack Schultz had the 30-meter record at 82 feet. You had to land standing up and not touch the ground with your hand. The official 50-meter record stood at 163 feet for a long time but I marked Franz Elsigan's jump at 186 feet. Some others called it 170. He out-jumped the hill. Landed on the flat; shattered the tips of both skis.

*Hook France and Charlie Lapp assist injured Ski Jumper
Courtesy of The Buffalo State Courier Express Collection*

"The cross country race course ran nine miles on Trail Number 4. It started at the Poma lift in Big Basin and ended up here at the Administration Building. The record time was one hour and twenty-two minutes. There were no groomers. Art Roscoe would have us kids do it, one on snow-shoes and one on skis. There were ups and downs and it was tough on snow-shoes.

"It was so grueling that Art laid out another one around Red House Lake. It started behind the Administration

Building and went uphill, then down the out-run of the 30-meter jump. There were some horrendous spills trying to do that on narrow skis. He'd have a ranger shoveling snow on the race track where it crossed the road. That course was a little improvement.

"The Chapel Downhill Race Course was behind the ski jumps by the old fire tower. They eventually tore the fire tower down, cut it in two and used the two halves as judging towers for the jumps. The downhill had hairpin turns. It ran across the top of both the 30 and 50-meter in-runs, then straight down for a hard right to stay out of the woods and then left to stay out of some more woods. I won it twice. My worst fall; I smashed my watch and both skis. Lost my hat. I found it buried armpit deep in the snow. You had to win the Chapel Downhill three times to keep the trophy. Tom Torge eventually retired it. That trail was extremely dangerous and fast; stick your poles out and you'd touch trees on either side.

"The Bova Number 1 rope tow had an electric motor and when the rope was new it would twist. Anything loose you had on would get caught. I was wearing this new loose parka. Red France was ahead of me. I yelled, 'Red, hit the safety gate' He yelled back, 'What?' and sailed off. I hit the gate but the rope had a lot of momentum and it yanked me up in the air so I cracked my head on the top pulley. Had to have eight stitches.

"On Bova Number 3, fifty foot from the finish, the downhill course dropped suddenly and then immediately flattened and went over a bridge. If you missed the bridge and leaned too far forward you'd do a front flip into the crick, too far back you'd go over backwards.

"In 1957 they installed the Poma lift in Big Basin. Over there the snow held longer into the spring."

Here Ted grinned and motioned to Jim Carr in the audience. "Jim Carr used to take care of the Poma. When I was just a little kid Jim would let me drive over there to Big Basin. I could just reach the pedals with my tip-toes and still see out the window. He had to grease the wheel on the Poma and he'd always put too much on. It would drip on the seats and mess up your ski pants.

"Jim himself had these beautiful gray ski pants. They had elastic under the foot and fit tight so he looked real cool. I remember when we got movies of him in a racing crouch on Bova 3 with the seat split wide open and his long john's hanging out."

Bob Carr spoke up from a bench beside Jim. "On a wet spring day the tow rope would tear up a pair of gloves. Remember the metal rope grippers we used to have?"

Ted laughed and said, "They've got mine on display up at Holiday. If you've got one, they are worth a lot of money. I bought mine right downstairs here in Harry Kilburn's ski shop. I bought all my skis from him."

Bud Boyer (in trees) off the 30 Meter Jump

Here Ted seemed to take a step back and re-address his subject. "I started skiing at 3 or 4. Jumping at 6 or 7. On my first 30-meter jump, Darwin Boyer talked me into jumping with downhill skis. I had always skied the out-runs. This time I walked halfway up the in-run. He picked me up bodily, turned me around and said 'Ready?'

"I said, 'Ready as I'll ever be.' I went off the jump and fell. I fell two or three more times and then I started making it standing up.

"When I was little, Ma used to take me to Bova. I had to ride up behind her because the rope was too heavy for me to lift. Soon as we got near the top I'd turn out from behind her and bomb straight downhill. Mom wanted me to learn to turn so she had Art Roscoe take me over to Bova and he showed me how to snowplow and stem and everything.

"Here's a typical Saturday when we were a little older. Five or six of us Park kids, in the morning, we would do 6 or 7 jumps. We'd walk up carrying those skis that weighed twelve pounds apiece. In the afternoon we'd go over and ski Bova. Saturday night at Bova we'd play 'GAT,' that's tag spelled backward. We'd play in the trees and you tagged by whacking the other guy with a ski pole. Art Roscoe didn't like it. On the last run of the night, when the hill was cleared, we'd line up across the top. We'd come straight down and try to jump the 9-foot hole at the bottom. You'd wind up in it or over against the opposite wall. We finally built a lip and made it all the way. Art didn't like that either.

"A ton of skiers came out of Allegany State Park that had Olympic potential, great jumpers, downhill and slalom. We had no training, poor equipment. We trained ourselves. My first cross-country skis were downhill skis my dad sawed narrow. The boots were work boots nailed on by the toe so you could raise the heel. We didn't have any money, so for ski wax I'd steal paraffin off mom's jelly jars or I'd steal it out of the other guys' jackets.

"We'd ski free if we helped Art pack the hill in the morning. Otherwise it cost us twenty-five cents. A regular ticket was fifty cents, later a dollar.

"We used to paint the ski jump like a ski, a red strip down one side and a blue one down the other and joined at the bottom. We decorated it with pine boughs and hung up our big

ISSC (Inter State Ski Club) banner. People and cars would line up along the road; sometimes we'd have five thousand people.

Jim Mendell, Don Fuller and Darwin Boyer
At the Top of the 30-Meter Jump
Courtesy of The Buffalo State Courier Express Collection

"Art Roscoe drove us all over for meets in his '52 Chevy: to Glenwood, Paul Smiths, and Bear Mountain. We jumped at Midland, Ontario one time. It was a 60-meter jump. I was never comfortable over 40-meters. Highest I ever did was 65. I wasn't eighty-five pounds soaking wet and I drew the fourth jump. There was this long line of jumpers behind me climbing up the hill and no way out. Numbers 1, 2 and 3 were all Canadian Olympic jumpers. One went off and fell, two went off and fell and so did three. I'm scared but I'm not going to wimp out. I'll just stand up at the end and slow down. That's what I did and I made it.

"At Paul Smiths, everyone else must have known how long the course was because they let me be the only one to bring cross-country skis. They stuck me with it. But I came in third. All I could see was woods and more woods. I wasn't seeing any other skiers or officials. I thought I was lost but then I passed two guys and came to the finish. Paul Smiths offered me a scholarship to their Hotel and Hospitality program but I didn't want any of that. So now I just retired from a career in the restaurant business. I turned it down. Don't tell my mother.

"I've never told anyone else this but I think I might'a took a shortcut.

"We ski jumped in flexible, worn, leather ski boots on twelve-pound three-groove skis. We waved our arms in the air trying to gain distance. We'd build up the take-off to try to get altitude. But no longer. Now they never get more than 8 to 10 feet off the ground. They have skis apart to catch more air, their arms are at their sides and they guide themselves with their hands."

Ted concluded with a blissful smile of recollection, "We were up in the air longer. Air pushing against you felt like someone with a big sky hook was lifting you up on a pillow.

"It was great to grow up in the Park."

MAPLE SYRUP
WAYNE ROBINS

March 15 2008

This is the month the Senecas call "Moon of the Maple." Sap is surging up from roots to the branches and buds of the sugar maples in our Allegany State Park sugar bush. The Historical Society has been invited to watch the sugaring off and eat pancakes and maple syrup with Wayne Robins and Judy Thaler of Nature Ed-ventures. They run the Allegany sugar bush.

Wayne Robins receives a handful of Maple Sugar

My dad grew up in the country and he loved maple syrup. The way he talked about it, it sounded so good we kids couldn't help loving it. He told us about a hotel in the Adirondacks that was his favorite because for dessert they would serve you a whole dishful of pure delicious maple syrup.

Today, here in the Park, snow still covers the floor of the woods but the deep powder has melted away on warm days leaving only granular icy layers that make slippery walking. It was freezing last night but scheduled to go into the forties today. This pattern of alternating freezing nights and warm days is unique to the climate of Northeastern United States and nearby Canada and is essential to the production of sufficient sweet sap to make maple syrup. Allegany is at the heart of this sugar-producing region. Wayne, our guide, dressed in a nineteenth-century plug hat, plaid wool shirt and gum boots tells us, "One of these trees, growing in Asia, will not make maple syrup. Bring it here and it will. We are the only place in the world that makes maple syrup."

Now he leads us single file into the woods to follow a trail depicting the history of maple sugaring. First he takes us to meet "a friend" who enacts seventeenth century Seneca sugar making. This young man, he says, was an orphaned white boy raised by a Seneca family. Wayne speaks to him using sign language. The young man is dressed in a coat made of a Hudson Bay Company blanket. He wears a cap with the single eagle feather, Seneca style. He silently tends a fire. Nearby a pair of wooden snowshoes lean against a tree and a trade axe is imbedded in a log.

Wayne shows us the "V" cut the Indians used to incise the bark of a maple and the hollow sumac spigot that leads sap out of the "V" to drip into a dish gouged in a log or into a birch bark container. Wayne says, "Each family member would have a thousand containers."

A large wooden vessel constructed like a dug-out canoe stands by the fire to receive collected sap for boiling. "Can you guess how the Indians brought the sap to a boil?" he asks.

One of the twenty-or-so of us who were crowded around the fire, answers, "With red hot rocks."

"Right," says Wayne as he approaches his friend and somehow persuades him non-verbally to show us. His friend selects two sticks from a pile outside the fire circle and lifts a series of rocks from the fire into the vessel setting up a great hissing of steam and a bubbling roll in the sap.

Wayne Robins demonstrating "V" Cut

"Mostly women did the sugaring. The men would be off hunting but they'd want to hang around and join the fun. One of the things they did for fun was pour syrup on snow which made a caramelized form of sugar, a tasty chew."

I remember Dad telling Grampa's story about how up in the woods they called it "Wax on snow." While they were sugaring they'd make some for themselves. Once in a while one of the dogs would sneak in and grab some and have a terrible time trying to chew it.

Wayne goes on, "the Indians had no containers to store syrup so they boiled theirs down into sugar. They ate great quantities of it straight, as sugar and cooked with all varieties of food: venison, fish, beans, corn, squash. They carved out little wooden molds in animal shapes and poured melted sugar into them. If you visited at their house you'd be offered one of these for a snack."

Grace Christy as a Settler's Wife Hauling Sap

Wayne turns to his Seneca friend and asks for some of the contents of his leather traveling pouch. Then he shows us the kernels of parched corn and chunks of hard maple sugar from the pouch. "These would sustain an Indian for food on a long journey," he says.

The small molded sugar pieces immediately bring to my mind a recollection of Dad taking us out to Cyril Murphy's farm near Orangeville to buy sugar and syrup. Cyril's wife, his sisters and his mother would be out in their steaming kitchen working over the wood stove boiling down syrup and pouring it into molds. We kids could hardly wait till the sugar cooled enough to be dumped out on the kitchen table and offered to us as soft, warm samples.

Settler's Sugaring Camp

The trail to the next stop on Wayne's historic maple sugar expedition leads up a treacherous slope towards an eighteenth century European Settlers camp. A rope tied to trees along the path makes the climb safer. He warns us that if we lose our grip we may wind up back in the fourteenth century. Along the way, Wayne explains, "During the Revolution the Senecas fought on the side of the British. To punish them, General Washington sent General Sullivan into Seneca territory and drove them back to Fort Niagara. The Senecas had large cornfields, apple, pear and peach orchards, storehouses of corn and lived in log cabins. Sullivan and his men laid waste to it all. The Senecas call that 'the winter of starvation.' After the war the new United States Government had no money but it rewarded its soldiers with grants of land here, on the frontier."

Our next sets of enactors are in the roles of a Revolutionary war veteran and his wife. The wife can't fool me; she looks a great deal like our Grace Christy, the Park Naturalist, unless she is her great, great grandmother. She wears a white bonnet and a green great cloak as she stands in front of her tent not far from an iron cauldron boiling sap over a fire.

Boiling Sap in Iron Kettle

Grace's enactor husband, also bundled in a great cloak but wearing a floppy wide-brimmed felt hat which often obscured his face, shows us how they had improved on the Indian technique of sugaring. "Indian sugar," he said, "was smoky and full of ashes and bugs. Boiling in a metal pot improved this, but was slow." Here he pointed to a cauldron and then to a smaller pot hanging from a tripod of saplings, "but boiling in a series of pots cut down boiling time and kept the product cleaner."

Wayne points out the settlers' use of wooden sap-collecting buckets hung from metal "Spiels." "Settlers found that cutting into trees killed a lot of them so they changed to using an auger. They drilled holes and inserted these hollow metal spiels to tap trees. Spiel is the New England nasally way of pronouncing the word spill, the common English term for any hollow tap into a container," he explained.

"Hanging buckets on a tree keeps them from getting kicked over or leaves and dirt blowing into them."

"Grace," he said, "show the folks how you collect buckets." Grace gracefully donned a wooden ox yoke and hooked buckets from either end to show us this 16th century labor-saving device. Then she pointed out the wooden sled with a barrel mounted on it for the same purpose. Wayne said, "They would also have a big horse-drawn sled."

Instantly I was back at Murphy's farm. Cyril was up on the mud sled holding the reins to his big brown horse, Shakespeare. A gigantic galvanized tank of raw sap rode behind him. "Sonny, come up here," he says to me, "You want to drive Shakespeare?"

Did I? You can bet on it. That was the thrill of a lifetime, driving that big horse through the bush down to the steaming sugar shanty to pour a load of sap into the evaporator. I had to struggle to keep from interrupting Wayne and Grace by yelling, "I drove one of those sleds."

Wayne interrupted my reverie to demonstrate the introduction of tin buckets and the invention of the tin can in the late 1800's. "Maple sugar was an important trade commodity for both the Indians and later settlers. After a time the US government removed tariffs and cane sugar imported from the West Indies became plentiful and cheap. But there was still a market for the delicious syrup with its characteristic flavor. Sugar could be stored in wooden barrels but not syrup. Barrels need to swell and syrup can't do that so syrup eventually leaks. With the invention of the tin can there was a way to bring syrup to the market."

Student sneaks a Sip of Sap

    A little further along the trail he points to covered galvanized buckets of the 1930's, flat shallow evaporator trays, ugly, leaking plastic bags of the forties and the, now common, maze of plastic tubes tangling a section of our bush. The tubing has certainly simplified moving sap from tree to evaporator shed but when we stop to look at it I have to comment, "Those tubes sure mess up the woods."
    Wayne agrees.
    We clamber downhill out of the trees and jam into the little building labeled "Sugar Shack." Steam billows from its windows. Inside we toast ourselves around the "arch" (metal box) that contains a blazing wood. Sweet fragrant steam rises

from the sap that circulates in a series of evaporator bays set on its top. A geezer inside, almost as old as me, tends the fire. Wayne stepping into the World War II time frame of the shed starts off with him, "Did you hear about the big battle on Guadalcanal Island?"

Sugar Shack 1940's Style

Wayne has me back at Cyril Murphy's farm during the war. Dad and I loaded up the trunk of our car with pound boxes of maple sugar and gallon jugs of syrup for our own pancakes and for Dad to sell to the other guys at work.

Wayne brings out a war time rationing book with sugar coupons and explains, "During World War II there were shortages of everything. Sugar, meat, butter and gasoline were rationed. So the demand for maple sugar went way up. There were so many little sugaring operations that the government couldn't control them by rationing but they did put price and sugar-content regulations into force. The price for syrup was $1.50 a gallon. I heard one place they are charging $48 a gallon now. Sugar content was set at 66%; Vermont always thinks it's a little better so they set theirs at 66.5%."

Now I realize Dad wasn't just reliving his boyhood in the country on those trips out to Cyril's place. Our family, guys at work and their families needed sugar and Dad was supplying it. Where we got the gas to make those trips to the country, I'll never tell.

The Cook

After the Sugar Shack, we all trek down to the Camp Allegany dining hall. There Judy and the kitchen crew have pancakes and sausage sizzling on a huge grill. I can see big juicy blueberries peeking out of some of the pancakes; Rick Feuz brought us a bucket of blueberries he picked in the fall. On each table are two pitchers of the succulent amber fluid of which we have learned a great deal today, pure 66% sugar-content Allegany State Park Maple Syrup. We hunker down and eat.

CHOIR CAMP AT CAMP CARLTON ALFRED KARNEY

January 2012

In all the times I've been to Allegany State Park I have never been to Group Camp 10, Camp Carlton. And now, before I've gotten a chance to see it, the State is talking about replacing all the old buildings.

Alfred Karney

As a camper my loyalty was always with Camp 12 which served first as the German-American Buffalo Turnverein Camp and later as Camp Arrowhead. Going south on ASP 2 toward Camp 12, I eyed that unknown place on a hillside to the west and wondered what went on there. Finally in January 2012, Alfred Karney, a longtime camper from Camp Carlton, volunteered to tell us its story at a Historical Society meeting. It was different.

Bob Byledbal Waiting for the Presentation

Before Alfred got going, Bob Schmid passed around notes from his newspaper search. Camp Carlton was built in 1925. It was the first Group Camp built on the Red House side of the Park and its buildings were the first wooden cabins in the Park. Previously, the accommodations were pyramidal World War I army tents. Camp Carlton had 12 cabins, a mess hall, ice house, shower, swimming pool and a playing field. From its opening until 1977, it was operated almost continuously as an Episcopal camp, first for boys, later for boys and girls. Since then, it has been available to the general public though often closed for repairs.

Alfred, who makes it clear that he prefers to be called "Alfred," is a balding heavy-set middle-aged man, about six feet tall. He wore sweat pants, an Allegany sweat shirt and, often perched forward on his nose, heavy-rimmed glasses. It is not easy to square that image of him with the colored snapshot of the nine-year-old choir boy in vestments which he displayed among his exhibits... until he rolled out his story and glowed with pride. The image clarified miraculously as he sang for us, albeit at a considerably lower pitch than in the old choir days at Camp Carlton.

Alfred Karney in Choir Vestments and Wearing Awards

Alfred began, "Camp Carlton was run pretty much like any other eight-week summer camp for 8 to 16 year-old children except that the first week was Choir Camp. The first of July 1961 was my first day there. I was eight years old and it was my very, very first time away from home except for grandparents. From July 2-8 I was homesick. I wanted to go home. I wrote a letter to my mother asking her to come and get me but the Choir Master stole it. I came back for six more years and I loved it and I've been visiting the Park regularly ever since.

"Choir Camp was not a babysitting service. It was semi-professional choir instruction with singing up to the standard of some of the best church choirs in England and the United States. Cecil A. Walker was camp Choir Master and responsible for much of this good work. Though he was born in 1910 and I in 1952 we were the closest of friends. Cecil had no boys of his own so Dave Smith, another choir boy and I, were like his own. We were both in the room when he died at age 71 in 1981.

"The Episcopal Church Choir Camp began in Ohio. In 1956 it moved from there to a camp on Lake Erie and in 1957 came to Camp Carlton. Western New York Anglican Bishop, Lauriston Scaife, was instrumental in locating the camp here and he rescued it when it almost collapsed in 1965. Every year Cecil Walker would order choir awards from England and Bishop Scaife would award them on the last day of camp at Saint Stephens Church in Olean. Reverend William Bowker, Father Bill we called him, was full time in camp every year from the 40's through the 70's. He used to collect the fire crackers that kids brought to camp and on the Fourth of July he'd set them all off.

"How good was Choir Camp? It was very good. Choir Masters were invited from all over the country, some of the best: Alec Wyton from Saint John the Divine in Manhattan, Thomas Mathews from Tulsa, Ronald Arnatt from Saint Louis, Alistair Brown from Utica, twice. And they wrote and used some top notch anthems while they were here. The Choir Camp belonged to the Royal School of Church Music founded in England in 1927 to which Choirs like those at Saint Paul's in Buffalo, Saint Patrick's Roman Catholic Cathedral in New York and Saint James in Orlando belong.

"We were taught to, as Cecil Walker would say so often, 'Sing with spirit and with understanding,' with mouth open, raised head, watching the conductor, projecting our voices and singing in crescendo. We would enunciate consonants and be careful of effects. I knew nothing about singing when I came here and Choir Camp taught me to sing. We had naturalists and they taught us nature. The Historical Society has taught me history. For two hours a day, we had choir practice. We were taught when to breathe and when not and we learned to sing."

Alfred then stopped talking, threw his head back and sang for us in a deep resonant voice: "Let them all rejoice in endless Hallelujahs."

We applauded. Then Alfred went on to describe and demonstrate briefly Gregorian Chant, the essence of which is that many words are sung on a single note and yet each word is not enunciated the same. His example was "Take my spirit with me." He added in an aside to us, "That's 'spirit' not 'Sprite', like a can of pop."

Alfred's singing was more polished than his humor though he deserves credit for trying.

"At Choir Camp we had a point system; 2 points for attending, 1, if you were late. The choir master watched us perform and added or took off points for singing with your mouth open or chewing gum. He would ask questions and award points for correct answers: "What is the name of this hymn? What years did Bach live? Name hymns that end in a minor or a major chord. We would be invited to his cabin to sing for from 1 to 5 points. At the end of camp we were awarded ribbons of various colors depending on how many years we had been at camp and how many points we had accrued."

Here Alfred proudly showed us a framed display of all the ribbons he had acquired. "We were allowed to wear these ribbons over our vestments back home together with the medal of Saint Nicholas, the patron saint of the choir boys of the Royal Society of Church Music.

Alfred Karney's Choir Awards

    He seemed then to have finished what he had to say, formally, about Choir Camp and started to fill in some of the details of camp life. "The kitchen was located right behind where we had choir practice and was often staffed with giggling girls. A very frequent call during practice was, ' Kitchen girls, please be quiet.'

Once Wolfie, Alistair Brown's dog, was out there in the kitchen and every time Alistair sang out 'Rejoice,' Wolfie howled.

"We'd get up at 7:30; have breakfast at 8, cleanup 8:30, inspection 9. We'd line up at attention and the camp counselors would come by to praise us or holler at us depending on how good a job we had done. We got points for this, too, and the cabin that did best got a watermelon at the end of the week. We had 80-90 kids in camp divided into 'A Chorus' meeting at 9:30 and 'B Chorus' meeting at 10:30. The rest of the day was swimming, archery, nature, arts and crafts and pioneering. In pioneering we learned how to not get lost and how to make a fire without matches, which never worked. And we had 'Store' where we could buy candy, pop and T-shirts."

Alfred then draped a Camp Carlton T-shirt that was designed for a 10-year-old over is his own full frame. I think he said, "It doesn't fit any more so I'm donating it to the Historical Society."

"We had baseball and water carnivals and at 5:30 chapel at Saint Williams-in-the-Wilderness. We sang at the evening service. Then supper, evening recreation, campfires, choir at 8:30 and bed at 9:30. Of course no one went to sleep. Who needs 10 hours sleep?

"I remember the counselor trying to get us to sleep telling the scary story about Bloody Mary coming down the mountain opposite camp and before she got to the end we eight-year-olds were sound asleep.

Alfred paused, picked up a stack of Xeroxed music and began distributing sheets from it. He then led us all in singing the hymn, "Evening," which sets a restful tone of oncoming night in the forest. I thought we sounded very good.

We gave him enthusiastic applause and gathered around to look over his souvenirs.

SPORTS CAR RACING ON RED HOUSE LAKE
BRUCE PERRY

February 2004

Bruce Perry spoke to the Allegany Historical Society on February 21, 2004 on the subject of Sports Car racing on Red House Lake. He brought along Ken Hogue who showed us a film clip of the racing. Bruce was kind enough to provide this copy of his talk for distribution to those unfortunate enough to miss the first hand presentation.

Red House Lake
Courtesy of Bruce Perry

Hi, I'm Bruce Perry and I have <u>no idea</u> how Larry Beahan found me. But I do know a bit about cars on the ice at

Red House Lake and at Larry's request I'm here to talk about it.

Bruce Perry, 2012

I'd like to introduce my wife, Beverly, and Ken Hogue. Among the three of us, our ice trial involvement covers practically every event from the first to the last.

Now if you've come here for tales of Dale Earnhardt on the ice you're going to be disappointed. I know the press release in the "Bradford Era" said I'd be delivering stories of stock car racing on Red House Lake, but it's not quite that spectacular. However, for 14 years we did run cars, one-at-a-time, against the clock, for trophies and a small amount of glory. It was generally great fun and good entertainment for ourselves and many spectators. It was also, for those of us who drove, an eye-opener as to how cars handle on very slippery surfaces.

Our club was the Allegheny Valley Sport Car Association (AVSCA), jointly headquartered in the Olean-Bradford area. It was founded in 1959, at the height of the sports car/ foreign car craze that was sweeping the country. This was the time when two strangers eagerly waved at one another because they were both driving sports cars on the same highway.

We all read "Road and Track" and "Sports Car Illustrated." We followed the races at Watkins Glen. We ate and slept sports cars. You just had to join a sports car club, to be with kindred spirits and to enjoy your car in friendly competition. Our club was, I must say, much more egalitarian than some. Our members drove everything from Porsches to pick-ups (Maybe this was due to our semi-rural heritage). Most sports car enthusiasts were not racers and our club, like most others, provided a safe competitive, legal form of auto sport through road rallies. And we held them almost every month. The events proved very popular and our club grew and matured. My wife and I really enjoyed rallying but I felt that the club should also pursue other, different events to compliment the rallies. Maybe something to perk up the members' enthusiasm in the dead of winter. I was president of the club at the time. I had heard of cars running on ice. Maybe we could do it. We certainly had the winter. I had two great super-enthusiastic friends in the club, Herb Good and Bob Potter. I broached the idea to them. The more we talked about it, the less insane the idea became. As the conversations grew more intense we became convinced we could pull it off.

There was one problem though. Just where would we hold this event? Why Cuba Lake seemed like a natural. But you'd have to get permission. "From whom?" said we.

Why it was under the control of the Allegany State Park Commission. "Who was ultimately in charge?"

"Leigh Batterson."

Well, we contacted him and set up a meeting. We called and immediately found our Cuba Lake was out: Ice fisherman, ingress and egress and other difficulties. But he mentioned maybe we could talk about Red House Lake.

Herb was called away on business, so it fell to Bob and me to meet Mr. Batterson face to face, with this rather nutty proposal. We wanted to impress upon him that we weren't some kind of juvenile speed maniacs so we donned suits and ties and tried to look like relatively responsible 30-year-old family men.

Waiting to Race
Courtesy of Bruce Perry

We were bowled over by his enthusiasm. It would be another new winter activity for the Park! The only thing that worried him was insurance. The club did have a million dollar liability policy underwritten by Lloyds of London. I don't know if it was Lloyds of London or our business suits but we began at that meeting a great relationship that lasted for years. A date was set: Feb 23, 1964. Forty years ago! As my mother once told me, "The older you get, the faster time goes by."

Anyhow we now had permission, a location and a date. Now we had to organize and promote the event. Our club was very good at promotion and publicity flew. The State Park workers plowed the parking lot and a route to the lake, providing planks for the cars to make the final transition onto the ice.

It fell to Bob Potter and me to lay out the course and a hundred other details. It had been a hard winter with a lot of snow on the ice and we had to establish a course. Bob knew a guy named Sonny with a kind of homemade Jeep (He said it was mostly Studebaker) who would be willing to plow any course we wanted--- for $25. So Bob and I and Sonny and a few other club stalwarts showed up Saturday afternoon, the day before the event, to make up an ice trial, which none of us had ever actually done before!

Oh yes, there was one other small detail, which we hadn't bothered to communicate to Mr. Batterson or anybody else. Neither Bob nor I nor anybody else we knew had any idea how thick the ice had to be to support a car. As I said, it had been a cold bitter winter and we were sure there was enough ice. Besides Sonny didn't seem to be worried so, lets go ahead and plow. I can't remember the exact course but it was kind of kidney shaped maybe a fifth or a quarter of a mile in length. Sonny didn't fall through. The ice seemed hard and stable so we each took our cars out for a couple of trial laps then went home to await the big day. We were now in it up to our ears. There was no turning back.

I did not sleep longer than 10 minutes at a time the entire night. Every time I shut my eyes, visions of cars plunging through the ice or similar disasters bedeviled me. Bob and I were to meet at the lake around 9:00 that morning. I think I was there about 7:00, and I decided to walk the course.

I ended up running off the ice in near panic. If the ice cracked once, it cracked a dozen times. These were piercingly loud cracks followed by a kind of a pinging sound. Bob, who also had not been able to sleep, arrived just as I was coming off the ice. He ventured out and heard the came cracking, the same pinging. What were we going to do?? Was it safe? Despite the cracking, the ice seemed solid.

As we dithered with our dilemma, our potential competitors started to arrive. In fact quite a large number were showing up. We had to let them in on the problem. After much talking, wailing, gnashing of teeth, one of the competitors said "Why don't we chop a hole in the ice and see how thick it really is?"

1966 MG Midget on the Course
Courtesy of Bruce Perry

A tire iron and a hammer were produced and after considerable effort we managed to punch a hole in the ice. The thickness was 16 inches. (I now know that would support a small locomotive.) The cracking seemed to stop as the sun got higher in the sky. Another competitor opined that maybe the sun had contributed to the cracking. So we opened registration and subsequently had a marvelous day on the ice; some 47 competitors with nary a mishap. The fastest time of the day was turned in by a Corvair from Buffalo, and each car got three runs.

By the way, we found out later that six inches of solid ice will support a car. We generally looked for seven inches, although one year it was closer to five inches. In all 14 years of running we never had a car go through the ice.

The success of the first running meant we now had an annual event. We were delighted and the Park personnel were also happy. So it was easy to schedule a second event for February of 1965, the second annual AVSCA Ice Trial.

However, try as we might we couldn't beat a January thaw. Up until the last minute, we hoped for sufficient ice, but it was decided on Sunday morning to run a gymkhana (or as they're called now-days and autocross) in the Red House parking lot. We only had 25 cars. But it was great fun and our club had now run it's first autocross. A type of event that became very popular a few years later.

From 1966 on we ran on the ice every year, although the 1966 event was touch and go until the last minute. But it turned out very successful with 54 cars. I think that was the year the ice was the thinnest. I think it was also the year that Bob Potter crawled out on the ice on his stomach to reach a young boy who had fallen through, near the island. He successfully reached him only to find the boy was standing on the bottom. His parents hadn't even missed him.

For 1967 we were able to schedule two events and we finally had cooperative winter weather which led to over 50 drivers at each event. At the second running we inaugurated our first ladies class.

At this point, I probably should elaborate a bit on the car classifications and the ice trial regulations. At the first event it was just two classes, based on engine size. Then their competition realized that cars like Corvairs, VWs, Saabs and others with engines over their driving wheels were usually faster. So we ended with four classes based on engine size and whether the engine was over the driving wheels or not. In the early years we did not allow 4-wheel-drive and you could not use studded tires. This class setup worked well for a number of years but change did come, as you'll hear later.

But the competitive spirit could not be kept in check and various participants schemed on how to gain an advantage but stay within the rules. There was the question of adding weight for traction. There was the high or low tire pressure debate. There was a move to snow tires on all four wheels and then there was tire compound, sawdust or steel filings in the tread. Then somebody discovered "siping" which was 100s of tiny knife cuts about an eighth of an inch apart on the tread of each tire to gain more traction. As I remember there was a shop in Salamanca that was very good at this. At least one team came up with a movable wing over the rear bumper of their VW. I don't think the car went fast enough for it to work.

1966 MG-b on the Ice
Courtesy of Bruce Perry

Another factor that really confounded things was the ice itself, and the days temperature. Sometimes the ice was fairly dry and had some traction. Sometimes it was slushy, sometimes it was covered with water and extremely slippery and sometimes all three conditions happened on the same day. Many days the ice got slower as the day wore on but occasionally it got faster. Very early on we realized that the fairest way to award trophies was the best combination of two times (usually out of three runs allotted to each car.) Then there were some drivers who, while making a Banzai run, would stuff it into a snow bank, which requires much pushing by the course workers, and sometimes a Jeep with a tow rope. <u>Unpredictability</u> was an inherent part of running on the ice.

In 1968, we again ran two very successful events. The fastest time of the day was set by a 427 Corvette. Ice running was hard to predict. This led to our scheduling three events in 1969. Due to mild weather the first was run in the parking lot but the remaining two were held on the ice.

For 1970, we again scheduled three trials which were all run on the ice. The popularity of these events was growing by leaps and bounds. The second event attracted 82 drivers. This was the first year we had a class for 4-wheel-drive vehicles.

In 1971, three events were scheduled but only the first two were held. Warm weather washed out the third running that year. There were 77 drivers at the first event.

1966 Sunbeam Alpine on the S Curve

For 1972, we got permission to run four events but it was one of those winters! We weren't able to run the two February events. But we did get in both of the March runnings. Turnout though, was way down because of the recurring cancellations. It was the year of our smallest entry lists, around 25 cars per event.

In 1973, four trials were scheduled, but we were able to run only two. And in 1974, we again scheduled four events but we were able to run only one. The ice was covered in a thin layer of water. We had 45 drivers and many said it was the slipperiest ice ever.

1975 brought a return of real winter. We held three events with good turnouts, the final event attracting 78 drivers. This was also the first year for a studded tire class (two wheel drive cars only).

1976 was probably the best year we ever had. The winter was cold. The ice was good and we had record turnouts 88, 86 and 60 drivers for the three trials. It was the last year that I drove. I won a second place with my 2-wheel-drive Suburban in the big car class. It weighed over 5000 pounds. What a ways we had come from not knowing how much ice would support a car.

1977. We were able to get in only two events, 67 drivers in the first and 52 in the last. The fastest time of the day, in event number one was a 4-wheel-drive Jeep, in the second a front-wheel-drive Saab.

1978. All good things have to come to an end. Our club was imploding. By that time the ice trials were our only truly successful events. Membership participation in all our events was extraordinarily small and the club was nearly dead. At the same time an aggressive new club, the 4-wheel-drive club of Bradford, was growing in popularity. Some of its members were also AVSCA members. They'd been enthusiastic in supporting our ice trials in past years and wanted them continued. It seemed logical that if the ice trials were to continue, they carry on the tradition. By that time I wasn't active in the club so I can't say how the actual transfer took place but it did. We loaned them our watches, pylons and other equipment and they continued holding <u>our</u> event for another seven or eight years. Ken was a participant in most of these and perhaps he can fill in some of the details.

In researching these trials I've been disappointed to find so few pictures but fortunately Ken shot a Super-8 movie in 1971(I believe) which should give you a little flavor of what it was like.

Ice-Block Racing Trophy

After you've viewed the movie, Ken, Bev and I would be glad to answer whatever questions you might have.

I must say after all these years, it was fun researching long ago events.

Thank you for inviting us to share it with you.

PART THREE

PLACES

ALLEGANY FIRE TOWERS

October 2005

Its fall and I yearn for the smell of burning leaves. Cider presses are running, pumpkins are popping up and maples are showing off in orange and red. I'm just back from the perfect place to watch that show, the top of the Summit Fire Tower in Allegany State Park. The rolling forested hills are breathtaking as is the 90-foot climb up the tower's wooden stairs.

The Beahans at Tuscarora Tower in 1934
Larry on left, Marj at right Mom and Aunt Laura Center

The first time I climbed a fire tower was in 1934. Dad never liked heights and Mom was not an adventurer, but my two-year-old sister, Marj, clambered all the way to the top before they could stop her. Mom and Dad had to go up to rescue her. I went along, not willing to let that little scamp outdo me. She still crows about it.

In the 1920's the State built four fire towers in the Pa
Firestorms had raged in the Adirondacks triggered by po
lumbering practices that left lopped-off treetops as tinde
covering the forest floor. Rangers manned the towers were and
watched with binoculars for smoke. They phoned in compass
bearings to locate the fires by triangulation. Today there are
small planes flying about, everyone has a cell phone and there
are many more roads.

Lyn Beahan Top of Summit Tower Oct 2005

Climbing the towers for the view became a tradition among campers. Former fire tower ranger, John Bryant, said, "One day I happen' to be on the tower, a group of children came up with a rather large dog. They all climbed the tower along with the dog. When they started down, the dog refused to go down with them. I finally had to carry him."

Summit Tower

Allegany rangers were usually men but a woman, Anastasia Flanagan Gray, is the most famous. During World War II her husband, who manned the Summit Tower, died. Manpower was short so Anastasia took on the job. Her granddaughter, Mary Jones, said, "She never had to deal with any major fires in the Park, but there were often fires along the river on the Seneca Reservation. Up in the tower, she h round table with a map on it covered with glass. She didn't any instruments. She'd just eyeball the location and th phone it in. I remember the phone with a crank on it hangin on the wall in the cabin.

"Once we were playing on the steps of the tower. Gramma was up in the cabin on top and couldn't see. A bear came out of the woods and started up the stairs after us. We were dodging from platform to platform and encouraging him, 'Here bear, come here bear.' She got a little upset about that."

The towers fell into disuse and disrepair. Then, five years ago, the Adirondack Mountain Club and the Allegany State Park Historical Society got together and held a Restore-the-Fire-Tower meeting in Salamanca. The fire hall overflowed with people and out of that grew the Fire Tower Restoration Committee. They sold T shirts and Fire Tower Patches to raise money and publicize the cause. The Park Administration joined in and Senator Pat McGee came through with enough money that volunteers have been able to restore the tower.

The final push came this summer. Former Park Forester, Terry Dailey a man who's training does not allow him to enjoy the smell of burning leaves as I do, he, with the assistance of a few hardy volunteers personally replaced every nut, bolt and board in the tower and then painted it. The restoration is not complete, but the tower is safe to climb.

Go on down to the Park, visit the tower for the view and for a souvenir bolt from the old tower. There's only one bucket of bolts left but the view will go on as long as the forest does.

ELLICOTTVILLE

May 2003

Oh! To be in Ellicottville now that May is here.

Church in Downtown Ellicottville

That fifty degree morning the sun shone brilliantly in a pure blue sky. Its light electrified the green hills, still swatched with snow, that back the brick stores and white homes of nineteenth-century Ellicottville. Winter crowds of skiers had evaporated. Summer leaves and heat had not yet arrived. We were there to greet the new season with hikes on Allegany State Park's rugged trails and strolls through sweet countryside and town.

Laidlaw House in Background

In this shoulder season, we had our choice of quaint and historic Bed and Breakfasts but settled on the modern luxury of the Inn at Holiday. A three-story fieldstone fireplace in its cathedral-ceilinged lobby stunned us. We magnanimously entertained tent-camping friends there in the indoor-outdoor pool, the sauna and the hot tub. In turn we were entertained by muskrats hurrying across the patio in front of our room. And the price was right.

The Niagara frontier Chapter of ADK organized this Finger Lakes Trail Conference gathering of outdoor enthusiasts. We allowed for wide tastes in the excursions offered. Athletes among us clambered through dark forests on the way from the Pennsylvania border ten or more miles over Allegany Mountains. We of more temperate spirits walked Ellicottville itself.

Routes 219 and 242 run together to form Washington Street, Ellicottville's hotel, restaurant and boutique-lined downtown. This crisp morning was "Great American Cleanup Day" across the nation and here as well. Dozens of volunteers, armed with rakes and black plastic bags, were giving the Town Hall and Historical Building a facelift. Most of the people in town were warmly dressed against the chill. But one old guy leaning on a broom wore only a baseball cap, tee-shirt and shorts. He spoke to us, "Too bad you didn't come on a week day. They only open the museum weekdays, when nobody is here. There's nothing worth seeing in it anyway."

Fall, as well Spring, is pretty in Ellicottville

The Ellicottville Historical Museum

We laughed and he was so pleased that he telephoned the curator. She hurried downtown to open shop for us as we returned to Washington Street for lunch. The building itself is tiny, made of brick and topped with an out-sized bell tower. It had been a bank, a Volunteer Fire Department, a German protestant church, the County Clerks office and some other things. The arrowheads, old uniforms, doll houses and sepia-toned photos of scions of the logger-baron Weller family were interesting, even more interesting then the volunteer, who had arranged our visit, implied.

I can't say I was stunned by the scrapbook-making class on the third floor of the Town Hall but it was an attractive old brick building and the people selling the scrapbook-making materials treated us to chocolate covered sponge candy.

The town, named for Joseph Ellicott, Holland Land Company surveyor, was founded in 1808. It was the seat of newly-formed, timber-rich Cattaraugus County. The town's glory still lies in magnificent trees. Full-bodied white pines and hemlocks tower along the streets and in yards. One gnarly oak has bark ridges raised six or eight inches off its trunk to mark its antiquity.

Visitors Center 9 West Washington Street

Ellicottville's lawns are a joyful bounty of green things, billowy coverlets of tiny blue flowers and here and there a bold golden dandelion. These lawns are to my taste. They are not made of suburban pesticide-ridden pool-table felt. They are real live green stuff and flowers, the perfect setting for homes like the Greek Revival house that banker Truman Coleman built at 43 Elizabeth Street in 1840. This square white domicile with its four columns and second story modeled like the Civil War gunboat Monitor is a striking example of the tradition and originality of this town.

Fifteen West Washington is the house that most captured my interest. Sam Johnson, a land agent, built its first section in 1846 as an office. A residence was added a few years later and then a school for the family kids. Late in the 1800's the owners took American chestnut logs, stripped them of their bark and set them as four pillars supporting the front portico. At first sight I thought hippies had engineered a quick repair of the house just a couple of years ago. But these rot-resistant logs, of trees that used to grow bountifully here but can no longer be found, have supported that roof for over a hundred years, without a coat of paint.

Geri Ciprich, our sainted leader, dutifully stopped in front of each building and read its history from the self-guided tour brochures she obtained for us. Most of the time we were in front of the correct house.

She was excellent in engaging townspeople to amplify the printed information. She got the janitor, or he might have been the pastor in mufti, to let us into Gothic Revival, Holy name of Mary, Catholic Church. Geri asked a woman working in the yard of her lovely old home, "Is your house on the Historic List?"

She answered, "No we've put on too many additions. And the place Speaking of eating, Geri then led us off to Dina's, downtown. There we rounded out the day with a magnificent lunch. I can personally recommend both the lemon meringue pie and the pecan-covered sticky buns.

is really a wreck."

I asked this lady if she knew anything about the beautiful but decaying horse-drawn lumber sled in her front yard. She said "I have no idea, that's my husband's doing."

But she did have much to say about the playful tom cat rubbing against our legs. "Poor guy has a heart murmur. It doesn't stop him. He's a bird murderer. I watched him grab a humming bird from the air the other day, and eat him."

WOLF RUN
DEBBIE MINA

April 2011

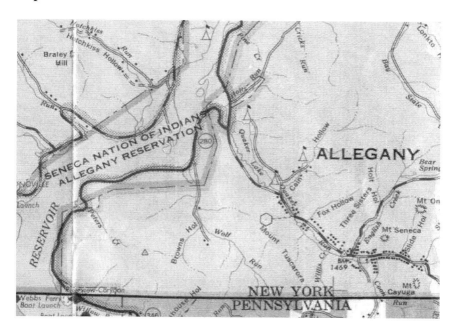

Wolf Run South of Quaker Lake

On the way from Buffalo to Allegany State Park today the April winds were howling. The radio forecast proclaimed a wind advisory, 50-60 knots, heavy rains and temperatures in the 40's. My new Subaru Forester is six inches higher than the old Subaru I just turned in. I had to do some careful steering in the heavy gusts. The air was cold, snow lined the roads in the higher elevations, there were uprooted trees and Red House Lake snarled with the first white caps I'd ever seen on it. The rain was light on the way down but a wind-driven drizzle had started by the time I reached the cozy warmth of the Red House Administration Building.

I was sure the hike to Wolf Run would be canceled, but just in case, I had brought boots, polypro underwear and Gortex foul weather gear. I checked with Rick Feuz, our Allegany Historical Society Program Chair and he said, "No. I promised Debbie Mina we were going and we are going."

Debbie Mina, 2012

Debbie Mina was the speaker for this meeting of the Historical Society. She is a slim lively woman of a "certain age." She wore hiking boots and pants with racing stripes and an Adidas emblem. She told us that her great, great grandmother, Louise Zibble, married Delos Carnahan in Ohio in 1847. They moved to Steamburg New York near present day Allegany State Park because of the plentiful lumber. He ran a saw mill there then took on the job of caretaker for the 8,500 acre estate owned by railroad millionaire Amasa Stone. On August 17, 1853 they were the second family to move into Wolf Run and while there Delos built the house and barn for the Stone estate.

Wolf Run is now an infrequently visited, remote section of the Park located off Highway 280 a little south of Quaker Run. Debbie commented, "They called it 'The Valley'."

In studying her family genealogy Debbie became fascinated by the old Carnahan Cemetery in Wolf Run. Her grandfather gave her directions, "You go to the culvert and look for three pine trees and then one."

"He was going to go up with me in the spring," she said "but I was in such a hurry I went up by myself in the winter. I was driving a new Firebird and put the first scratches on it."

She passed around photos of headstones and a 1907 Carnahan reunion saying, "One of the headstones is for a woman born in 1800 who lived to 1906."

William Zibble marker Carnahan Cemetery

Debbie had an obituary for Delos Carnahan from December 27, 1897 and a 1915 map of Wolf Run with all her family names. She said, "There are believed to be at least 40 burials in the old cemetery. Today there are only eight marked graves. One bears the name Glen C. The story is that he was only twelve. His mother sent him down to the station on an errand and he was killed by a train. Another marker is for William Zibble. Checking Civil War records I found that he had been granted a Veterans pension in 1890. I am trying to get a GAR (Grand Army of the Republic) marker for him."

Wolf Run School 1902

In introducing Debbie, Rick mentioned that one of the markers in the cemetery was for a woman born in 1800 who had lived to 1906.

I can't help my own associations to stories like this. "My grandmother Beahan kept on her bedside table a picture of a Union trooper holding a musket across his chest. I finally found out that he was her cousin Uncle Charlie Royce, wounded at Bull Run. After the war he and his wife settled land out in Ohio. We were able to trace the movements of his regiment the 94th New York Infantry, the Belle Jefferson Rifles and come pretty close to figuring out the situation they were in when he took a bullet in the left arm.

Uncle Charlie Royce

Debbie has her great, great grand mother, Louise Zibble Carnahan's diary, kept from 1903 to 1955. "It tells of their daily life. One day they picked blackberries and drove down to the station to sell them. They had quilting bees and did knitting for soldiers during the war. There were notes on the weather and on fixing fences.

"I like to think about what their lives were like up there with no electricity or plumbing. I have their old kerosene lamp. They had to use an outhouse. My copying machine sits on top of Louise's beautifully carved table. I wonder what she would think."

Debbie showed us the name of one of the Carnahan girls in a copy of the graduating list for Chamberlain Institute, a young ladies' finishing school at Randolph, New York. The school was founded in 1850. Its hilltop site is now occupied by Randolph High School. "I never thought Louise would have the money to send her daughter to a place like that," she said.

Debbie's thoughts put me in mind of Gramma Beahan. I have her diaries, she always mentioned the weather, and often described dances where, "We had a big time." Her father was on the school board so the school teacher often boarded with them. Imagine living with your teacher. I was surprised to read that my skinny old Gramma, one day on her father's wind-blown farm up on Tug Hill, dug a whole wagon load of potatoes.

Even when she was married and I visited her and Grampa they still got water from a pump and had no electricity. They heated and cooked with wood. There was always a stack of wood in the back yard and part of the fun was helping to chop the big blocks into stove-sized pieces. The best thing I ever tasted was Gramma's homemade bread toasted on her wood stove and soaked with butter. And they had an outhouse equipped with a Sears and Roebuck catalogue for reading and whatever.

Debbie recalled reading a newspaper piece from 1903. She said, "I know you park people don't like to talk about rattle snakes. This was a report of a man from Wolf Run who came into town with thirty rattle snakes in a box. The article advised, 'Don't go down there in hot weather.'"

Debbie's mention of rattle snakes reminded me of a friend's experience. She was walking in the Park near Bee Hunter trail when she noticed a rustling in what looked like a pile of leaves at the edge of the path. She snapped a picture and got out of there quick. When the picture was developed she was amazed to see that it was of a coiled rattle snake. I looked up timber rattlers on the internet, when coiled their brown and gray stripes do look a great deal like a small pile of leaves. The US Fish and Wildlife service describes the Northern Timber Rattler as a candidate species for its threatened and endangered list.

She went on, "I found an article from the Rochester paper in 1901 saying that they had discovered oil on Ralph Carnahan's farm in Wolf Run." She asked if any of us had information on oil wells out that way. I was busy with taking notes or I would have told her that there were more than 200 oil and gas wells in Allegany State Park, some of them still active and that gas exploration still poses a terrible threat to the Park's forest.

Debbie halted there and asked for questions. Hook France, a former Park Ranger who grew up and still lives in the Bay State Area of the Park, was sitting in the front row next to me. He volunteered, "My dad got me my first pony from Harry Carnahan up in Wolf Run. I was there the night the big barn burned down. The guy who had the contract from the Park to take down the houses was probably taking a short cut with the barn."

That resonated with Pete Smallback, a dairy farmer and Allegany History buff whose father bought the farm at Tunesassa after the Quaker Indian School closed. "I remember the house fire up there," he said, "Charles Carnahan had been at a funeral and left the place untended. That's how the fire started. They had to get out of there so quick they were throwing their belongings out the second floor window." He also recalled, "When we were hunting up there we'd stop at Vince Carnahan's. His missus would cook for the hunters."

Hook added, "A couple of elderly women came into the station. One of their fathers was a railroad section hand in

Wolf Run. She said she remembered the Carnahan men, 'They scared me to death. They all wore big straw hats, went barefoot and had a lot of sheep.'"

Debbie said, "I always thought William Carnahan was a little crazy in the head. He had a team of horses he was working with up in the woods. Every morning he'd stick the point of his knife down into arsenic and eat a little bit of it. Then he'd give some to each of the horses. I read somewhere that doctors used to prescribe arsenic for indigestion. So maybe he was on to something. He also used to line his boots with straw which we thought was strange but we found out later that Indians used straw like that for insulation right along."

Wolf Run Lumber Mill Crew

Bob Schmid had done his usual careful preparation for today's subject. He distributed a CD of old Wolf Run photos and maps and a 1955 newspaper article by Frank Carnahan, an old Wolf Run resident. It is three full columns of stories and facts available on the Internet at:

http://www.rootsweb.ancestry.com/~nycattar/pioneer/wolfrun.htm

Grampa Beahan and his Lumber Crew

The photos were of Wolf Run homes and mills, a class outside its one room school and a crew of workmen posing outside a mill. Frank Carnahan recalled forty families living there. The JM Bemis Lumber Mill employed sixty men. One year there were ninety teams hauling logs to them. He described a practice of forming logs into rafts and the men floating them down the Allegany to sell at Pittsburgh. Several families used to get together to cut their winter wood in a wood cutting Bee. They'd fell trees, saw them into chunks and split them for burning. They'd work all day; have a big supper and then a dance.

And I recall the photo that hung in my grandparents' dining room. It was of Grampa Beahan and his 1904 Adirondack lumber crew.

Nowaday you rarely see anyone in Wolf Run. It is meadow and young woods returning to forest, an important wild part of Allegany State Park. My most enduring recollection of the place was when, in 1997 the Park made a mistake. They allowed the National Muzzle Loader Rifle Association to stage a week-long "Primitive Encampment" of 2500 people in 36 acres there. These would-be mountain men built fires, cut trees, constructed corrals and parked their cars in those acres and, as might be expected in Allegany, it rained.

Bulldozer at the Muzzle Loader Rendezvous

Here is the scene as I described it then:
Imagine for a moment the Erie County Fair held in a swamp, or Woodstock on the way to becoming the Confederate prison camp at Andersonville. You're getting close. Imagine a hoard of congenial, well-meaning locusts intent on having a good time, descending on a meadow in four-wheel drives, while it's raining.

They made a terrible mess of the place. I don't think they will be back.

Wolf Run gradually heals its wounds. Brush replaces grass. Trees spring up. Rattlers sun themselves on rocky outcrops. Deer graze and the occasional black bear wanders through in hope of a berry dinner. A trace where the railroad track passed can still be seen on aerial views and the old cemetery remains with its eight headstones. The footprint of man gradually disappears from this serene valley.

Meanwhile the Historical Society meeting had lasted till 3:30, the rain kept pouring down but Rick, Debbie, Tom and one or two others were still bent on a hike to the Carnahan Cemetery, despite their cotton clothing. Where I come from, they call cotton dungarees, hypothermia pants because cotton stays wet forever and when wet provides no insulation.

Carnahan Cemetery, Wolf Run

Debbie told me, "No problem, I used to be a mailman." I looked at the rain and remembered times I had been wet in the wind. There is no colder cold than wet cold out in the wind. One time my son Teck and I were camped on Fox Island in the Adirondack Stillwater Reservoir. It was Sunday afternoon. The rain poured and the wind blew but we had to get back to work. We paddled half way back to our car when lightning began to strike around us. We made shore and squatted in the best lightning defensive posture, freezing in the wind till the lightning ceased. I recall coming down off Mount Jefferson in

A new Headstone for Silas Nellis'

the White Mountains. Our party of eight had gotten lost on a new trail. Some of us were soaked with sweat despite the winter cold. My partner collapsed. We revived him with about a gallon of hot chocolate.

I desperately wanted to go along to Wolf Run but not in that kind of weather. I could not dissuade the other hikers. They persisted and reported having a good time.

As it turned out I was able to take some of these pictures on a trip to the Carnahan Cemetery a few months later. It was raining again but we were better equipped. On that occasion we helped Debbie mark the grave of Silas Nellis, one of her forbearers.

RED HOUSE INN

August 2005

On this sunny August day, we met in the St John's-in-the-Woods Chapel, the last of the old Allegany-style shuttered buildings in the Park. It is directly across the road from the Quaker Store Museum. We had hoped to meet at Charlie Dach's old Red House Inn just outside the Red House toll booth. But it was not possible because the Inn was in such a sad state of disrepair.

Red House Inn

Charlie is a tall, lean fellow with a full head of curly grey hair. He's quick with a smile and a handshake. On August 20, 2005 he returned to the Park for the first time since 1979.

That year he and his family gave up the park concession business they had run at Allegany for 43 years. It was not easy for him to bring himself back to talk to the Allegany State Park Historical Society about those years. As close as I could scratch it down, here is what he had to say:

Charlie Dach and Jim Carr 2005

"The Dach family came to Allegany State Park for vacations. We rented a cabin on Ryan Trail on a yearly basis in the 1940's. Dad had a meat market in Buffalo. It was in either the second or third ward, an old German neighborhood. He sold general groceries, too, and during the war he had access to ration coupons.

"There was an accident in the Park. One of the Park Commissioners had a daughter killed here in an auto accident caused by alcohol. The Commission outlawed alcohol sales and that almost closed the Park concessions. They had depended on selling alcohol to stay in business.

"Mom and Dad knew many people here in the Park including the Carrs. Dad's dream came true. They asked him to take over the concessions. Because of the war-time sugar shortage there was no Coke in the Park, even though they made it right over here in Bradford. Dad had enough sugar ration coupons to supply Coca Cola.

"Dad loved to cook. For a time, we had all the concessions in the Park. We ran the dance halls, weekends in winter the ski areas kept us as busy as the summer. We even catered for group camps, supplied the cooks, the food, everything. But the concession business was tough when you had to bid to operate them every three years. If you got the bid then you'd have to rush to get souvenir items made in time for the season. It was too much. So we gave away the rest of it and kept the Ad Building restaurant and gift shop---and the Red House Inn.

Red House Inn Barn

"My mom loved pine trees, particularly tall ones that haven't been trimmed and have branches that come down to the ground all the way around. In 1955 we bought her the house behind the row of pine trees, just outside the Red House entrance. The house was security against losing our contract more than it was a place to live. It became The Red House Inn.

"We advertised it as a Tea Room but lunch and dinner were the mainstay. Mom wanted a rose garden for weddings and formal affairs. The paneling was pecky cypress from some old barn in Louisiana. I remember scrubbing off the moss with a wire brush. We used chestnut from the West Coast. The parquet floors came from Rochester. She dragged me around to every known store to pick that out.

"Why was it painted red or pink? Because it was the Red House Inn.

"We had the grand opening in 1957. I didn't remember the date. I got it from Bob Schmid. What I remembered was that it was the year Ozzie Schultz fell off the second floor of the Inn. Dad delayed the opening a year. He wanted all the bugs out. One man died of a heart attack opening day."

Here Charlie paused. Then looked up and said, "It wasn't the day. He was going to have it anyway.

"We operated from noon till 8pm. There were always long waiting lines. Meet the Millers of Channel 4, if you are old enough to remember them."

The audience laughed as several of us were indeed that old. "They came down and gave us a plug several times. I guess they are working up a dish or a meal somewhere up there now." He gestured toward the sky. "The old Buffalo Courier gave us good write-ups too.

"John Peters, 'Gramps,' was 72 the day he came to work for us and he was 72 when he left twenty years later. He knew roses, their character and their soul. We got them from Wyatt-Roses in Ohio. I don't think they are around anymore. Our perennials came from Cherry Creek. Every year Dad would take the old blue-grey Willys out there and load it up with flat after flat of seedlings. We used ground corn cobs for raised beds. Bob Schmid showed me a newspaper article that said we had 750 working plants at a time. I don't think, in fact, it could have been more than 350.

"One year Gramps tried a new formula for the flower beds. It contained ground bone. The next morning half our plants were dug-up by raccoons wondering where the bone odor came from.

"The Red House Inn was known for great food and we had great employees. They knew everyone that came in. Some came once a week, some once a month and we knew them by name. Kids had the bonus of taking a bun out to feed the horses.

"Everyone who came in and sat down got a starter tray. It had herring, cottage cheese, bread sticks and two kinds of relish. The herring was famous. It was Aqua Herring we bought up in Buffalo. The same kind you can buy today but no one believes that when I tell them. They say, 'It don't taste the same.' I never realized we had so many Danish herring-lovers around here.

"The salad tray was a big old brass tray from Mexico. It held several tossed salads, each with a different dressing. And there was the pink mayonnaise for Jell-O."

Here Charlie hailed Mercy Holliday, one of his old waitresses, out in the audience. "Mercy, don't you go telling them how someone left cherry juice in the mayonnaise bowl and we were too cheap to throw it out." Mercie and all laughed.

"We had one person maintain contact with a customer through the whole meal. The same person would take the order and bring the food. Not like today.

"Esther Schultz made pies for us that couldn't be beat. My brother claimed her pumpkin was best." Here he paused, then went on with a grin, "But he never tasted the apple. We had turkey. We bought beef by the side. Dad cut up the beef and he never cut the same way twice. We'd use every bit of it in one way or another.

"The Ad Building restaurant worked hand-in-hand with the Red House Inn. If Red House was busy Alice would come down to help out and bring along some turkey."

He waved to Alice Altenburg in the audience and she waved back.

"It was not fast-food. You'd come in and spend some time. Everyone wanted a table by the window. Mom loved picture windows and she saw that they built in six or maybe it was seven of them.

Mercy Holliday and Alice Altenburg, Red House Inn Waitresses

"With all the weddings and motor coaches we had coming we planned to expand. Mom wanted a circular building with a rotating floor. It was her dream. But it never happened. The day our builder filed for a permit, we discovered that we did not own the land.

"The deeds were picked up and in 1967 the Park bought us out. The Park people were awful tight about it, too. For instance, they bought our walk-in coolers but they wouldn't buy our compressors. Finally those three-year contracts hurt us so we divorced ourselves from the Park. What hurt most was when they cut down all those pine trees at the Inn. Mom used to make ceramic owls and we wired them up out in the trees so when customers looked out they'd see the owls blinking at them. The trees hurt more than tearing out the rose beds.

Moose in Administration Building Restaurant

"Why did we locate the Inn at the Red House entrance? Route 62 used to be the main route from Buffalo to the Park. On 219 there was a steep hill coming up out of the Cattaraugus gorge and the old gravity feed cars had to back up the hill. Then when they got off 219 on to ASP 1 it was a dirt road, a long, long tunnel of trees.

Administration Building Restaurant Classic Dishes

"Basically, my parents found a place they loved and where they could make a living. For me, it was wonderful to grow up here. I came back even though my wife warned me that as a result of my wild childhood here, Hook France (retired park policeman) might still have some open warrants out on me.

"What was my favorite thing about the Park? The day after Labor Day was what I liked best. The day THEY went home. Of course the weekend before Memorial Day I couldn't wait till you all got down here."

That got considerable laughter from the crowd.

"The worst thing I remember was Friday nights, loading garbage into the old blue-grey Willis and driving it up to the Red House dump. Sometimes the road would be lined with cars of families going up to see the bears. And we'd sit in line and wait and wait, in the heat with the garbage stinking. And I would be planning a date. I knew I'd have to take a shower and change clothes.

"Dad's worst thing was lugging coal in and ashes out of the Administration Building. There was a dumbwaiter we could have used but it went through the Park Police Office and the pulley was so weak that once you loaded it the ashes would just crash down into the basement.

"People come up to me now and say 'Don't you remember me.' I say 'Sure.'

"How long were we there? ---Forty-two or three years. We left Easter 1979. Dad worked 18-20 hour days. But then he'd take us on vacation. He always had a Buick Roadmaster, for the big trunk. I remember going to the Grand Canyon. All the Indians came down to meet Dad with their mule train and he'd be buying up souvenirs to sell.

Charlie answered many, many questions. After a while I tried to cut them off with the idea of his taking the group out to the Inn just to look around the grounds. But questions kept flying at him. He kept on answering. Finally I got a chance to make my suggestion. He declined saying, "Last time I looked in the window of the Inn there were old mattresses piled up in the dining room. I don't think I could take it."

Then he concluded, "I recall the charm of that whole era. Mercy and Alice were there working with us. In the fall the leaves would color up and the motor coaches would come rolling in. Folks would come in laughing and leave laughing."

Charlie got resounding applause and fell into laughing conversations with many old friends as he worked his way out of Saint John's.

BUZZARDVILLE

January 2004

Red House Administration Building in Winter

"Do you know what Buzzardville was?" Pat Sheffer, a retired Buffalo grammar school principal and longtime denizen of Allegany State Park asked us. Nostalgia turned her into a girl again and belied her graying curls. We twenty listeners had gathered in the paneled great room of the Red House Administration Building to hear her and her older brother, Bernie, answer that question. Bernie is a burly ex-railroad signalman. Completing the picture, but threatening to steal the show, three deer grazed on bird seed in the deep snow outside the bank of French doors.

Deer outside Administration Building Great-Room French Doors

"Buzzardville was two big white farmhouses and two small cabins just outside the old Quaker Run entrance to the Park," Pat said. "Bob Banks owned them and the little one-pump gas-station-store down the road. The Park has expanded to include them now but the driveway is there and the Park still mows the lawn where our flagpole stood and where we used to play baseball. Quaker Lake covers the site of the road. And of course the old Quaker Bridge across the Allegany River is gone.

"From 1946 to 1953, my folks rented a cabin on Kaiser Trail for two months each summer. In those days the yearly people, like on Buffalo Trail, were allowed to rent year-round. They added rooms and porches and fireplaces. Some of their cabins still have those improvements.

"The last Friday night dance of the season was supposed to be a Dawn Dance. It didn't go to dawn, just to 12 instead of 11. But after the Dawn dance of 1953 we moved to one of Bob Banks' farmhouses and rented it year round. We cleaned it all out and scrubbed it down with bleach. There was an outhouse. The stone fireplace was huge. It could warm the whole front of the house. The window glass was so old it was wavy and there was a beautiful old gas stove in the kitchen with the oven up on top. Oh, I wish I had that now.

Buzzard

"When I got up that first morning and went out to use the outhouse there was the biggest buzzard I ever saw sitting on the roof. I called my sister and she was petrified. If you moved, it just followed you. We went inside and came out the front and there was another one. They were Turkey Buzzards, ugly critters and they stayed especially close.

"Someone, who shall remained unnamed, got a rifle and popped them."

At this point Bernie Sheffer, who is well known for his hunting prowess, beamed but continued to let his sister do most of the talking.

"Next weekend we had a party at the new place. All the German Village people and the yearly people came down. One of our friends had painted a sign with a big cockeyed buzzard saying "Hic." And everyone got a pin with a buzzard on it. Bob Banks hung up that sign for us and took care of it for years.

"There were always parties at Buzzardville. You couldn't buy beer in the Park. Bob Banks' store was the first place outside the Park where you could. Saturday night someone at Mooney's Bar would announce, 'Party at Buzzardville and it would be like Margaritaville.'

"Roland Remington's farm was nearby. He used to keep live trout in his milk house. Shea's had a log cabin. The Attea's had a place. There were lots of kids around. And in our yard there was a wonderful gazebo with roses climbing over it. The ground cover all around was periwinkle and there was a beautiful larch. When the larch first turned brown and started to lose its needles I thought it died. Then I found out that larches aren't like pines.

"The big tree where the road curved was struck by lightning. The lightning used to come right through the mountain and down the valley hitting trees. You could taste it. Bob Banks said one strike near the store knocked all the tacks out of the floor. Everyone had lightening rods on their cabins and we were all afraid to use the rabbit ears on our TVs.

Bob Banks' Store

"His store was our library. There was a table and chairs. On a rainy day when the pool was closed we'd go there and read magazines for hours and never buy anything. He made the best chocolate milkshakes in the world. We wanted to pick blueberries up in Cain Hollow but he warned us about the rattlesnakes up there.

"Banks had his own big gray cottage down the road further. He'd come by every morning on his bicycle. He was a golf professional, worked at Cherry Hill in North Carolina in the winters. He'd go over to Bradford to buy steak to sell in the store and leave someone else in charge so he could play golf. He left in 1965 when the Park expanded and took over his store and Buzzardville. No one has heard from him since.

"That was the year my dad retired from the railroad. He loved it so, he would have lived there. Loved to fish. He and my uncle would get up at 4:30 am to go down to the river and fish. I begged to go. My uncle finally said 'Come on, get in the car, but you have to be quiet.' It was so beautiful and quiet down at the river. The deer would come down and sometimes it was so shallow they could walk right across.

"Dad went down there the last weekend before the Park took over. October first Banks came, said goodbye and turned off the power. He didn't say anything to anyone, but when he found Dad, he turned the power back on and Dad stayed there till December.

Here Bernie came in with, "I was down on the river early one morning. Watched this doe come walking down to take a drink. 'Bang.' Seneca, standing up on the bank, shot her and came down to get her out."

Pat resumed, "We used to come down in the winter to ski. The snow we brought in on our boots would not melt all weekend, it was so cold. In the summer we would organize the campfires in the Park every Saturday night. It was just an ideal life. I cannot think of a better place to have spent my summer youth than Buzzardville."

CEMETERIES IN THE PARK
HUGH DUNN

October 2008

"Hugh Dunn is the newest member of the Allegany State Park Commission and a former NY State Parks, Allegany Regional Director," announced Rick Feuz on introducing him. "He is going to tell us about cemeteries in the Park."

Family Marker in Wolf Run's Carnahan Cemetery

Hugh did not just talk about cemeteries. He wandered through forty years of Park experiences.

Hugh is a stocky, vigorous man; some, including Hugh himself, I believe, would call him pugnacious. But this day, as he addressed us in his old stomping grounds, the Red House Administration Building, he wore corduroys, a woolen shirt and a broad grin.

Hugh Dunn 2008

There were forty people in attendance eager to hear him; one of the largest assemblies the Allegany State Park Historical Society has had at one of its programs.

Hugh had to share the limelight with Ken Pierce, a Salamanca native who is better known in the rest of the world than in Salamanca. Ken is a world champion quick-draw, knife and hatchet-throwing performer who has been seen in many movies and has had a regular act in Las Vegas. The two were old pals. Ken freely offered recollections, from the audience. But Hugh held his own in the exchange.

As he began, Hugh announced that he had worked in the Park for forty years doing everything from Engineering Assistant through Red House Manager and he felt honored to be named a Commissioner now. "When I started, I felt proud to be an Engineering Assistant." Here he took a breath to blow himself up. "Then I found myself assigned to picking up papers on ASP 1." He deflated with a grin into a slump. "Jim Carr was with me." Here he indicated Jim in the audience. "We didn't worry about job titles, we got the job done. After I was promoted, I never liked to sit in the office and cover my tail writing papers. I'd get out and dirty my suit. I had a management style I called "Managing by Wandering Around."

"I was fortunate to work here. Doors opened and I took advantage of them.

"I know we have had some differences of opinion here, but the biggest disappointment of my life was that we never got a Park Master Plan. The 65,000 acres of forest was my concern. After I retired, I was hesitant to speak out for a long time; I was so shaken up by the Master Plan. When I did finally speak here a couple years ago, Doctor Beahan," pointing to me (author of this article), "said 'You are one of us.' I am. I'm a conservationist, a bird lover. I love the Park and I don't want us to love it to death."

Hugh brought to my mind years of struggle between conservationists, the logging industry and the Park management over this Master Plan that might have authorized massive logging operations in the Park. Hugh and I were on opposite ends of that argument.

"November 12 I'll be 80 years old," Hugh said. "Eighty years old, I can't imagine that.

"I have been picking people's brains doing research about the Park for years. Why keep it to myself. I'm here for you to pick mine.

"There's a rock over toward the Bay State area of the Park, in the valley just beyond Old Baldy. Old Baldy that's not bald anymore. Carved on that rock is 'Igman 1880...

something.' I have been reading Charles Congdon's book, *Allegany Oxbow,* and he quotes a Doctor Larkin's writing about 'the Little People,' 'Go up Igman Hollow, ' Larkin says."

I recalled my solo trip up Old Baldy.

In Fredrick Larkin's 1880 book *Ancient Man in America* he describes old baldy as a prehistoric hilltop fortress. I thought I could see remnants of a ridge around it where a palisade might have stood and unusual stone works at its summit. The mountain was once clothed in American Chestnut trees. They died of blight leaving it bald for a time.

Rock Structure on "Old Baldy"

"The Senecas clam up as soon as you mention Old Baldy to them. Congdon talks about it in his book along with copper fittings for wooly mammoth harnesses and those little people, the Mound Builders. No one has carried on research locally on their relation to the Senecas.

"There are monuments in the Park that go back to 1791. Over in the Rice Brook area, Little Ireland had a cemetery. I thought I had lost my mind when I was there last. Before, I had seen all these little tombstones, each with a little story. They were all Irish names. Some were little babies. When I went back they were all gone. I checked with Hook France. He remembered the little stones.

"All that was left was the huge Irving family tombstone. It was too big to carry away.

Little Ireland Rock Foundation

"There was an Irish family, ran a tannery in Limestone. They brought fifty families over from Ireland to settle in Little Ireland, near there, along Rice Brook. They all left to work in the oil fields during the boom. A few years ago an old gentleman came back to Little Ireland to look for some money he had buried. He died there. I think he just wanted to come home.

"There were a lot of Carnahans buried in Wolf Run, during the big logging boom. So it was called the Carnahan Cemetery.

"After all the hardwoods in the Park were logged-off, then the soft woods, they stripped the bark of hemlocks for tannin. Then they went for the small trees that were left. Chemical factories were built to extract alcohol from them. The land was selling then for as little as $1.60 an acre.

"When I was Director and the question of gas exploration came up, I wanted to save certain wild areas like the old growth hemlock in Big Basin. A lot of the mineral rights stayed in private hands when the State bought up land for the Park. I had them map mineral rights ownership and we found that it was up to 63% of the Park. The only thing we could do when someone wanted to drill for gas, was tell them where the roads could go."

Here, Hugh threw up his hands and then returned to the topic of cemeteries. "There was a cemetery in Red House. When the Reservoir was flooded they moved them." He pointed to Jim Carr in the front row. "Jim, your mother and father were buried there, weren't they?" adding, "Jim is a lifelong resident of the Park."

Jim said, "Yes they were. The graves were moved to Steamburg."

"At the new Camp Turner there is a little field with a bluff above it. In the field are 2 or 3 tombstones."

Bob Schmid held up his hand and said, "That was the Barton Family cemetery. There was a large one and two smaller ones last time I was there. One was for Leonard Barton, another for his son-in-law, Gideon Ceascy.

Hugh said, "The Park started with seven thousand original acres and gradually expanded taking in many homesteads, often with their own small burial places. The 'political' boundary of the Park includes sixty-five thousand acres but the State only owns sixty-three thousand of them. Most of the private in-holdings are over in Bay State and in Limestone. During my administration we bought about a thousand acres, mostly in Limestone.

Cornplanter's Monument at Corydon

"Bear hunting's not allowed in the Park. But there is no clear understanding whether that applies to private land inside the Park. Today, I stopped in the Park police office. They still don't have a ruling on it. If I were the judge I'd say it was illegal.

"Outside the Park, Cornplanter is buried in the Riverview Cemetery in Corydon. They had to move his grave from the banks of the Allegany on the Seneca Reservation when Kinzua Reservoir was flooded.

"Then there are the 'so-called' cemeteries. Dave Bemus showed me a place in the Park where there are several stones. People who were born here or just happen to love the Park, have their ashes brought in and marked with a stone.

Kenny Pierce 2008

Hugh said, "I've been asked about gold mines in the Park. There was one by Frontier Village the other side of the Summit and one on State Park Avenue not far from the Stone Tower.

"Larry Kilmer wrote a marvelous book about the railroads that ran through here. When we laid out the cross-country ski trails we used all local historic names. Patterson Trail that runs down over to Camp Allegany in Bova was an old railroad bed. Leonard, Ridge Run, Bova, they are all historic names. I think we should stick to history in naming places."

I'm not sure what switched Hugh's train of thought here but he smiled with this sudden recollection. "They used to find great big rattlesnakes in Wolf Run; bring them down to Red House beach and lay them out. They said, 'Up close they smell like cucumbers.'"

Here Kenny Pierce brightened up. He is a wiry older man with a thin angular profile like on an Indian-head nickel and a handshake like a steel vise. He wore a navy blue watch cap and a red-plaid flannel shirt. Earlier he had told us that he was in treatment at the Salamanca hospital for cancer but that he had just returned from doing a knife-throwing exhibition at the Alamo in Texas. He said, "My sister ran over a big den of rattlers with her car up behind Robinson Run. There were 17 little baby rattlers there."

While he had the floor, he told us that he discovered his grandfather in Congdon's *Allegany Oxbow* book, Abel Pierce. Abel had worked with Buffalo Bill, trained horses, and did Wild West shows, worked with Senator Fancher, the founder of the Park.

"Up till 1942 we Indians," Ken said, "weren't allowed to go to public school, neither black or red people. They didn't want us educated."

Here Hugh came back in. "And how about some new ideas for the Park. Let's give the kids a maple syrup education all the way from spigot up to modern techniques. Let them taste it, eat syrup off of snow.

"And pollution, Red House Lake is getting more and more polluted with those geese. Sooner or later they will have to cut off swimming. How about an Olympic-sized pool down behind the beach with a water park nearby for campers.

"The trails in the Park are in terrible condition. You can't hardly find Beehunter anymore. With a three-man crew and an ATV we could clean them up in no time.

Old Growth Hemlock in Big Basin

Lou Budnick asked, "What about the panoramic sites, the overlooks?"

Hugh said, "Like Fancher Point, we cut the trees out of the way and planted wildflowers. When I had my forestry crew we furnished firewood to every employee who lived in the Park.

"Prepare for this shock," Hugh said staring at me (the author). "How about a foot trail into the 350-year-old old growth hemlock in Big Basin?"

"Great idea," I responded.

"I know where one of the largest existing ash trees is, up toward Longtow Hollow.

"Not miles long," he said, "Show them what virgin timber looks like ... of course," he added facetiously, "when I built the ski trails they said, 'You didn't cut down a tree, did you?'

I raised an eyebrow, wondering what kind of thoroughfare he was thinking to drive through those sacred hemlock woods. He's a nice guy and he loves the woods but I'll have to keep an eye on this new Commissioner.

He got a good hand from the crowd as he concluded, leaving me with a vision of little people driving copper-harnessed wooly mammoths with pots of gold on their backs as they paraded down Main Street in the village of Red House still buried beneath the shimmering lake before us.

VILLAGE OF CATTARAUGUS
PATRICK CULLEN

March 2007

Patrick Cullen was to tell us the story of Cattaraugus, a village 13 miles north of the Park on Route 353.

Downtown Cattaraugus

He is a huge man and his ambition as founder and driving force behind The Historic Southwestern NY Foundation and the American Museum of Cutlery match his physique. It was Saint Patrick's Day when he addressed the Allegany State Park Historical Society and he wore an enormous green sport coat and green shirt. The tweed cap which he wore down over his eyes was just like ones worn by jaunting cart drivers I've seen in Cork.

Pat Cullen 2007 with Ka-Bar Fighting Knife

I'll try to tell you what he had to say:
The Irish had a good deal to do with putting Cattaraugus on the map. When in 1849 President Jackson decided to connect the Hudson River to the Great Lakes at Dunkirk, the Erie Railroad came through the sleepy little town of Cattaraugus. Suddenly the population grew from 30 to 4500 like Deadwood on the HBO TV series. Three railroad construction gangs were located there, two Irish and one German. The Cork Irish got to fighting the other Irish and this led to most Cattaraugus County deeds having in them a proviso that no alcoholic beverages be manufactured or sold on the land being conveyed.

Pat's interest in history began as a kid with rat shooting expeditions to dumps. There, coincidentally, he found many historic pictures and artifacts which he brought home to form his own museum. He has a love-hate relationship with museums and historians. A mismanaged museum with a leaking roof destroyed a precious photo collection of his. A museum director discarded all photos that did not have identifying data. Some mistaken historians base the Cattaraugus Village centennial on the date of 1882 while it is well known that its vibrant history goes back to 1810".

Cattaraugus Cutlery Museum

Here Pat distributed his own brief history of the Village.
"When the Railroad was completed two trainloads of important people including President Fillmore, Daniel Webster, the Seneca Chiefs and 350 others made a two-day trip from the Hudson to Lake Erie stopping along the way for speeches and picnics.

Soon Cattaraugus had apartment buildings, the largest axe factory in the country, a tannery and every imaginable tradesman. In 1831 a Cattaraugus banking partnership was founded, not on cash but on the IOU's of its directors. It was an ancestor of the current Bank of Cattaraugus, founded in 1882. This bank is now the third oldest bank in the U.S. Pat has been its president for 25 years and was preceded by his father who served in that capacity also for 25 years. It is the smallest bank in the Northeast with a capitalization of $1.5 million and with no interest in expansion. In fact, when nearby South Dayton wanted a branch of it in their town, one old woman depositor shouted, "Let them establish their own bank."

"We are happy with the local service we provide.

"I run this small antique gun shop in town. It's open two hours a week. A fellow brought in this map." Pat pointed to a large framed map. "I bought it for $20. On it, in the town of Napoli, I found the name Champlin. John Brown Franklin Champlin, founder of Cattaraugus Cutlery, one of the oldest cutlery companies in the area, was born there. The old house was still intact. We had it disassembled by an expert in post and beam construction. In the process he found a supply of grindstones used in the business. The house is ready for reconstruction when we have a place and the funds.

"Champlin was severely burned in a fire. When he recovered he was left so that he couldn't do farm work and his father set him up as a traveling tinker with a horse and wagon. Then the railroad came through so that locally-made products had access to world markets. A head of cheese made in Cattaraugus could be for sale on the streets of New York City in 24 hours.

"Champlin went to work selling scissors for Friedman and Lauderdale, a German cutlery firm. Then he borrowed from our bank and went into the cutlery manufacturing business here. He married Theresa Case. Several of her brothers, who were in trouble for selling horses to the James Gang, settled here and went into the business with him.

"From that, the cutlery manufacturing trade blossomed. Within a 50-mile radius 150 different cutlery companies existed over a 200-year span. Their production numbers rivaled or exceeded all other cutlery regions in the world including Sheffield, England and Solingen, Germany.

Local manufacturers paid transportation costs of skilled workers from those regions to Cattaraugus to man their plants. The Bank of Cattaraugus still numbers among its customers historic knife makers and their descendants.

Home of John Brown Franklin Champlin
Founder of Cattaraugus Cutlery

"There was no museum of cutlery in the U.S. or in the world. Our bank was the obvious sponsor for one. It took eleven years for the NYS Board of Regents to first approve our Historic Southwestern New York Foundation and then our American Museum of Cutlery. You have to know someone to get it done. We were moved from the bottom of the pile of 10,000 applications to the top when Robert Bennett, Chairman of the New York State Board of Regents, happened to be in Cattaraugus and we took him on a tour.

"So now we are an approved 501(C)3 corporation and we can accept money from anyone with an interest in any kind of historic preservation. We have the 1904 Palace Theater, the Cattaraugus Hotel and three or four other places ready to be restored. Your old lumber mill here in Allegany State Park would be a wonderful project worth preserving. Our Foundation could help raise money for it.

Alice Altenburg handles a Bowie Knife

I had a call from a fellow with a collection of 200 tomahawks that he wants to donate. We have one of the largest timepiece collections in existence, worth 2.5 million dollars but we need a building to put it in. We have a museum space of only 600 square feet and it's full. We are open four afternoons a week.

"We need volunteers to be there and write down the stories that come in, like the woman who recognized a photo of her grandfather. She told of his having been one of nine brothers who worked in the axe factory and formed their own unbeatable baseball team. Or the WWII PBY tail gunner who saw Pappy Boyington shot down and brought in a hunting knife manufactured in Cattaraugus. He wore it all through the war strapped to his leg to cut himself loose of the tail turret if he was shot down.

Pat had laid out a table full of knives for our inspection. They included several KaBar military knives, originals and ones modified for individual use and a celluloid-handled jackknife, but the prize was a Bowie knife whose ivory handle ended in a creature that was half-alligator half-man the way Jackson described the Tennessean volunteers who went to the Alamo. The weapon's bright blade looked like a combination Roman short sword and meat cleaver. He said it was worth $2000.

He rounded the afternoon off with a story responding to my question, "Do you have a knife that murdered anyone?"

"Did someone tell you that?" he jibed back.

I said, "No."

"In London in 1836 a woman was horribly murdered, shot, strangled and stabbed. They caught the guy who did it. It was a notorious case. They did a book about it. Even dissected his brain. But the knife disappeared.

"In 1937, someone was remodeling the house and down behind the plaster and lath they found a dagger. They figured, in a hurry to hide it, he stuck it in the wall. A soldier brought it back from England to Buffalo after WWII and sold it to me. It's a peculiar long knife with a wire handle; the book said it was an 18th century Spanish dagger. The cross section of its blade exactly matched her incisions."

We applauded Pat and plied him with questions while gingerly handling his collection of murder gear. We may be able to learn a few things from Pat and his Historic Southwestern New York Foundation. To start with, we ought to be thinking about preserving that great sawmill of ours.

PART FOUR

POLITICS

LOGGING

June 2005

Beware! A critical fragment of New York State's forests are open to timber harvesting---at the flick of a bureaucrat's pen. But if Assemblyman Richard Brodsky of Westchester can get his bill (A1803) into and through the New York State Senate, all forests in State Parks and all Old Growth Forests on State land would remain intact, for our pleasure, for our understanding and for the good of the earth.

Allegany State Park

The Assembly has passed this bill ten years in a row. The Senate has stonewalled it every time. We must find Senators to sponsor A1803. We must persuade them that there is no need to sacrifice these forest treasures held in trust for the people of New York, that the vast acreages of privately-owned forests which cover much of New York State are ample sources of timber.

Zoar Valley

My family "stompin' ground" is a stretch of protected New York woods along the Little River not far from the Adirondack's Five Ponds Wilderness. My Dad was born in a shanty on that river where Grampa bossed a lumber crew. Now, a hundred years later, the woods that Grampa turned into a moonscape have taken back the land. I trek in there with my kids to breathe clean air, walk among tall trees and canoe dark waters. Away back in there is a stand of virgin White Pine that Grampa and the boys never got to. You see that stand --- you'll catch your breath. Our neck of the woods is part of the New York State Adirondack Forest Preserve which, like the Catskill Preserve, is protected by the "Forever Wild" clause of our State Constitution.

Since Grampa's day we have learned that forests are not an inexhaustible resource and that they are essential to clean water and flood control. Recently the Max Planck Institute for Biogeochemistry showed that the earth's forests store enormous quantities of the greenhouse gas, carbon dioxide. The existence of forests may control the tipping point between a stable world climate and the catastrophe of global warming.

Tom Beahan's 1904 Lumber Crew

After the woods were gone, our family couldn't make a living in the Adirondacks. We moved and took up other work. But we stayed addicted to the woods. When we can't make it back up North we take to our formidable Western New York woods in State Parks, Forests and Multiple Use Areas. None of these enjoy protection from logging.

I live near Zoar Valley Multiple Use Area. The canyon that carries Cattaraugus Creek's white water through Zoar is spectacular and it conceals, in the shadows of its shale recesses, a wonder of Old Growth forest, a grapevine 12 inches in diameter, the world's tallest basswood (128 feet), the world's second tallest sycamore (153 feet), a tulip tree of 156 feet, a bitternut hickory of 136 feet, a white ash of 139 feet, and a cottonwood of 131 feet. Some trees there are more than 300 years old.

It was too tough for guys like Grampa to get down in there in the old days and extract that timber. Industrial strength helicopters have changed that. And logging is one of the uses prescribed for Multiple Use Areas of which Zoar is one.

Bruce Kershner in Allegany Old Growth Hemlocks

Alleghany State Park, just 70 miles from my doorstep in Buffalo, is 60,000 acres of 100-year-old second growth with a majestic 770-acre core of 350-year-old hemlock. On my bookshelf sits a several-hundred-page logging plan prepared by the Park. The plan includes a state-of-the-art sawmill. One option the plan offers would cut timber on 30,000 acres, excluding, at least for now, those 770 precious acres of "old growth." In response to massive protests, the plan was shelved by the State ten years ago. But that bulky tome has not faded away; it continues to hang fire like a by-passed land mine ready to blow the legs off any reasonable forest ecology policy.

New York State controls 650 acres of maturing forest that stands on a high slope overlooking the village of Perrysburg. In the distance, out across Lake Erie, you can see the mist of Niagara Falls. The forest floor, lumpy with moss-covered nurse logs, snags and rotting hollow trees, feeds woodpeckers and shelters fox, skunk, raccoon and squirrels. Its soil is mushy with last year's snowmelt and lush with trillium. It replenishes the aquifer that supplies drinking water to the village below. Its standing timber has been appraised at $1.5 million.

Forest at Perrysburg Hospital

Meanwhile the State Dormitory Authority struggles with the City of Buffalo over the sale of that pristine land. Buffalo originally owned the property and ran a tuberculosis treatment center tucked in a corner of this health-giving sanctuary. New York State took over the hospital operation but the City retained reversionary ownership. The City wants to keep the forest intact; the Dormitory Authority seems determined to sell it to a logger at the fire-sale price of $400,000. If that sale goes through and that watery slope with its Hobbit-like enchanted forest is crisscrossed by heavy equipment and denuded of trees, Perrysburg will be drinking muddy water, if not flooded off the map.

GAS

July 2008

Allegany State Park was once riddled with 200 gas and oil wells. Its forest has healed much of that scarring. But National Fuel owns a lease on 5000 acres at its heart impinging upon the 350-year-old Old Growth Hemlock forest. The gas and oil rights under half of the Park are in fact privately owned. Those rights, under current law, can be exercised whenever prices are right. With the tapping of Marcellus Shale's natural gas that time is now.

Gas Well just inside PA at Top of Allegany's Black Snake Trail

Already, just south of Allegany State Park in Pennsylvania's Allegheny National Forest, private owners of mineral rights are making plans to drill at the cherished Rimrock Overlook. The view of Kinzua Reservoir from Rimrock will be spoiled by roads, trucks and derricks destroying its forests.

The Marcellus Shale is a layer of porous rock, the size of the state of Florida, 6-8000 feet below the surface. It stretches across New York State's southern tier through Pennsylvania to Ohio. The current price of gas has set off a feeding frenzy of gas-leasing in Southeastern New York State and it is headed straight for Allegany State Park. Fortunes are being made as great stretches of forest, farm and park land are becoming contaminated industrial wasteland.

The quantity of gas in the Marcellus layer is estimated to be enough to fire the needs of the United States for one to two years. That quantity of energy is hard to refuse in these days of attenuated fuel supplies.

During the big oil boom of the 1890's there was a circuit-riding preacher who, on his rounds of the Pennsylvania and New York oil fields, would exhort against the exploitation of gas and oil. "The Lord stored oil in the earth to fuel the fires of hell," he warned. "To remove it is sinful and the world will feel His wrath."

And this old fellow had never heard of "Global warming."

If we burn all that Marcellus natural gas it will inevitably produce CO_2, trap more heat and contribute to the melting of our polar ice. The Marcellus formation requires very deep wells that must first be dug vertically and then run horizontally in order to allow 1 – 3 million gallons of a water-sand-chemical mix to be forced into the rock to fragment it and release the gas. The disposal of this waste water, its chemicals and the radioactive and other byproducts of the drilling will contaminate vast areas. A single well head will require hundreds of trucks servicing it daily. Aquifers will be drawn down and will risk contamination. Forests and farms will be cut up by roads and well pads.

Land owners may consider it their right to despoil their own acres in this way but we cannot let it happen to a sacred place like Allegany State Park. Call your State Legislators. Tell them to protect Allegany from the fuels of hell.

JULY 2009
APPEAL TO PARK USERS

<u>This is an urgent time for Allegany State Park.</u>

U.S. Energy has made application to start drilling oil wells in Allegany State Park.

You can help protect the Park by writing the Governor, your legislators, newspapers, DEC and OPRHP urging that they step in to protect this magnificent 100-square-mile Park. If we don't stop it here in Allegany we may lose many other Parks to this kind of wasteful exploitation.

Please mine the letter printed below for ideas or copy the whole thing if you like.

Suggested Addresses below.

<u>Act Now or Lose Allegany as We Know It.</u>

      Lovers off Allegany State Park, disaster is upon us. The mineral rights under half the Park are not state-owned. Albany has been repeatedly urged to buy them. Now the rogue oil exploration company, US Energy, of Amherst NY, claims title to 3000 acres and intends to turn Allegany into the oil field it was 100 years ago. Imagine Allegany's 100 to 350-year-old forest chewed up by oil roads and rumbling trucks. Imagine oil wells clunking in the hills. Imagine Red House Creek and the Park's drinking water with an iridescent oil slick.
      Shreiner Oil and Gas has already contaminated the water wells on Hedgehog Lane in Bradford, PA a couple miles

south, and are "hydro-fracing" oil wells there (the environmentally questionable practice of fracturing petroleum-bearing shale by driving tons of water down a well). US Energy, claiming mineral-rights ownership, is cutting timber and driving holes in the floor of the 8000-acre forest which is Bradford's "watershed."

Adirondack Mountain Club reviewing US Energy Co. Violations at DEP Headquarters in Meadville PA

On July 10, 2009 the Pennsylvania Department of Environmental Protection ordered U.S.Energy to cease all gas and oil exploration in Pennsylvania, for "persistent and repeated violations of environmental laws... the consequences being the contamination of water and soil in Warren and McKean Counties." Friends of Allegany, our worst nightmare is here. These pirates, U.S.Energy, have made application to drill 5 oil wells just north of the Pennsylvania border in the venerable Quaker Run half of New York State's Allegany State Park.

Park Authorities and the Department of Environmental Conservation assure us that they will force U.S.Energy to prove ownership of this first 3000 acres and any other, they try to access. Each agency will require a permit. US Energy must do a full Environmental Impact Study and Review under the State Environmental Quality Review Act. The agencies promise to demand the highest level of protection of surface rights. The Adirondack Mountain Club has appealed to the State Attorney General to review U.S.Energy's claims. But all this may not be enough to preserve Allegany's magnificent forest, intact.

Allegany State Park should not be sacrificed to a short term greedy petroleum fix. Its rocky headwater streams, eight old growth forests sites, ancient hilltop fortress, several Rare, Threatened and Endangered Species, 361 varieties of mammals, reptiles, amphibians and fish and its million and a half human visitors each year deserve better.

Gaswell at top of Black Snake Mountain

New York State must save Allegany from this petroleum monster by: 1. Eminent Domain to acquire all its mineral rights. 2. Protecting it under the State Natural and Historic Preservation Trust, Article 20 of the Park Law. 3. Enacting Sam Hoyt's bill, Assembly 9070, which sunsets unused Allegany mineral rights after 20 years. Contact the Governor, the Legislature, the DEC and Parks... or lose Allegany.

Mail your letter to or call:

Governor David Patterson, State Capitol Albany NY 12224
518 474 8390

Assembly addresses: http:/assembly.state.ny.us/mem/

Senate Addresses: http:/www.nysenate.gov/senators/

Commissioner Peter Grannis, NY State DEC 625 Broadway, Albany NY 122333
518402 8545

Commissioner Carol Ash NYS OPRHP Empire State Plaza Agency Building 1, Albany NY 12238
518 474 0456

Larry, Nick and Teck Beahan
Do not try this with real bears.